THE UPPER ROOM

WHERE THE WORLD M

Gift Aid item

20 **00007073862** 6318

Sarah Wilke
Publisher

INTERDENOMINATIONAL
INTERNATIONAL
INTERRACIAL

33 LANGUAGES
Multiple formats are available in some languages

The Upper Room
September–December 2016
Edited by Susan Hibbins

The Upper Room © BRF 2016
The Bible Reading Fellowship
15 The Chambers, Vineyard, Abingdon OX14 3FE
Tel: 01865 319700; Fax: 01865 319701
Email: enquiries@brf.org.uk
Website: www.brf.org.uk
BRF is a Registered Charity

ISBN 978 0 85746 400 2

Acknowledgments
The New Revised Standard Version of the Bible, Anglicised Edition, copyright © 1989, 1995 by the Division of Christian Education of the National Council of the Churches of Christ in the USA. Used by permission. All rights reserved.

Scripture quotations taken from The Holy Bible, New International Version (Anglicised edition) copyright © 1979, 1984, 2011 by Biblica. Used by permission of Hodder & Stoughton Publishers, a Hachette UK company. All rights reserved. 'NIV' is a registered trademark of Biblica. UK trademark number 1448790.

Extracts from the Authorised Version of the Bible (The King James Bible), the rights in which are vested in the Crown, are reproduced by permission of the Crown's Patentee, Cambridge University Press.

Extracts from CEB copyright © 2011 by Common English Bible.

Printed by Gutenberg Press, Tarxien, Malta

The Upper Room: how to use this book

The Upper Room is ideal in helping us spend a quiet time with God each day. Each daily entry is based on a passage of scripture, and is followed by a meditation and prayer. Each person who contributes a meditation to the magazine seeks to relate their experience of God in a way that will help those who use *The Upper Room* every day.

Here are some guidelines to help you make best use of *The Upper Room*:

1. Read the passage of Scripture. It is a good idea to read it more than once, in order to have a fuller understanding of what it is about and what you can learn from it.
2. Read the meditation. How does it relate to your own experience? Can you identify with what the writer has outlined from their own experience or understanding?
3. Pray the written prayer. Think about how you can use it to relate to people you know, or situations that need your prayers today.
4. Think about the contributor who has written the meditation. Some *Upper Room* users include this person in their prayers for the day.
5. Meditate on the 'Thought for the day', the 'Link2Life' and the 'Prayer Focus', perhaps using them again as the focus for prayer or direction for action.

Why is it important to have a daily quiet time? Many people will agree that it is the best way of keeping in touch every day with the God who sustains us, and who sends us out to do his will and show his love to the people we encounter each day. Meeting with God in this way reassures us of his presence with us, helps us to discern his will for us and makes us part of his worldwide family of Christian people through our prayers.

I hope that you will be encouraged as you use the magazine regularly as part of your daily devotions, and that God will richly bless you as you read his word and seek to learn more about him.

Susan Hibbins
UK Editor

In Times of/For Help with . . .

Below is a list of entries in this copy of *The Upper Room* relating to situations or emotions with which we may need help:

Bible reading/study: Sept 11, 13, 18; Oct 13, 15, 28; Nov 14

Change: Sept 13, 26, 27; Oct 1, 4; Nov 10

Christian community: Dec 25

Comfort: Nov 3, 7, 10, 30; Dec 5, 17

Compassion: Nov 13

Encouragement: Sept 3, 15, 27; Oct 9; Dec 10

Evangelism: Sept 24; Oct 3, 27; Nov 14, 17; Dec 4, 24

Faith: Sept 3, 8; Oct 16; Dec 30

Forgiveness: Oct 2, 10, 30; Nov 6, 19

God's goodness/love/grace: Sept 1, 28; Oct 2, 20; Nov 9, 15; Dec 8, 18

God's guidance: Nov 2, 3, 8, 20; Dec 13, 27

God's presence: Sept 5, 30; Oct 4, 25; Nov 9, 21; Dec 18, 31

God's provision: Sept 25; Nov 12, 21; Dec 8, 19, 20

Growth: Sept 7; Nov 10

Guidance: Sept 10; Oct 15

Heaven: Dec 29

Healing/Illness: Dec 22

Holy Spirit: Nov 11

Hope: Nov 27, 28; Dec 14, 17, 31

Justice: Dec 28

Joy: Oct 14, 24; Dec 18

Listening/Waiting for God: Nov 3; Dec 2

Living our faith: Sept 6; Nov 5; Dec 1, 2, 5, 26

Making choices: Nov 25

Obedience: Oct 5, 14, 21, 24, 31; Nov 17

Praise: Sept 29; Nov 4

Peace: Oct 18; Nov 1, 26; Dec 21

Perseverance: Nov 5

Prayer: Sept 9, 21; Oct 7, 26; Nov 9, 30; Dec 23

Renewal: Nov 10, 27

Repentance: Nov 6, 19; Dec 3

Salvation: Sept 5, 16, 19; Oct 31; Dec 4, 11

Serving others: Sept 3, 27; Oct 6, 29; Nov 4, 30; Dec 1, 16

Spiritual practices: Sept 2,4; Nov 23, 25; Dec 2, 31

Strength: Sept 17; Oct 9; Nov 21; Dec 19

Thankfulness: Nov 24

Truth: Sept 12; Dec 18, 26, 27

Trust: Sept 3; Oct 16; Nov 7, 11, 28; Dec 6, 9, 10

Unity in Christ: Oct 7

Worship: Sept 29; Oct 13

'Come to me, all you that are weary and are carrying heavy burdens, and I will give you rest. Take my yoke upon you, and learn from me; for I am gentle and humble in heart, and you will find rest for your souls' (Matthew 11:28–29, NRSV).

As a volunteer for The Upper Room's prayer line, Earl Fuller has taken all sorts of prayer requests by phone—about illness, death, job loss, family crisis. But this time, he wasn't prepared for what he would hear after his usual greeting: 'The Upper Room Living Prayer Centre. May I pray with you?'

'What did you say?' replied the voice of a young girl.

'This is The Upper Room Living Prayer Centre,' Earl repeated. 'May I pray with you?'

Silence. Earl waited.

The girl's voice returned, this time filled with excitement. 'Is this... is this... Jesus?'

At first, Earl chuckled. But then tears filled his eyes. How could he possibly respond to the hope and curiosity of this precious child? Finally, the words came.

'No, this isn't Jesus,' he said. 'But I am Jesus' friend.'

That was enough for the girl. She said her name was Brittany and she needed a prayer for a relative who 'wasn't in very good shape'. And so Earl prayed with her.

Afterwards, as Earl considered the girl's initial confusion, he kept praying. He asked for God to 'keep me humble. And when people call looking for Jesus, and they just get me on the other end of the line, they will still find him.'

It is my prayer, too, for all the volunteers who set aside their time to take the 800 requests we receive each day by phone or online. Surely, like Brittany, we are all looking for Christ in our lives, especially in times of suffering.

I'm grateful that The Upper Room's prayer ministry is responding to this need, helping those who call or write to find the rest in their souls that only Christ can provide.

Sarah Wilke, Publisher

Where the World Meets to Pray

Thirty years ago, I made my first trip to The Upper Room in Nashville, Tennessee. I have two memories of my initial visit. My first memory is of The Upper Room Chapel, bookstore and museum. Each helps make The Upper Room an honoured place of prayer. They are not unique in this, but they are special. The Upper Room ministry serves as a sentinel for what matters most in this life—a living relationship with our loving God. My second memory is of visiting the editorial offices. A sense of calm and grace was palpable. The people and the place exuded a spirit of prayer and concern for the common good. I will never forget that first experience which so clearly reflected the ministry of The Upper Room.

It is a privilege to make all of the resources of the Upper Room available 'Down Under', here in Australia. Whether it is the daily devotional guide, the work of the Emmaus Community, Companions in Christ, or the other excellent resources provided, The Upper Room is a total ministry—a ministry of deep prayer and spirituality. I stand on the shoulders of amazing people—Gloster Udy, Ray Hughes, Tony Nancarrow, Sarah Wilke and Steven Bryant, to name only a few. For many decades, The Upper Room has been a staple in the Australian spiritual landscape and has provided a sorely needed foundation of prayer.

We currently distribute about 4000 copies of the daily devotional guide. From the letters of appreciation, we know it is shared—passed around from subscribers to other readers—even more widely. I am equally excited about the opportunities that social media will offer in the future. We can only pray that technology will allow us to reach a new generation and establish new communities of prayer and devotion.

Here in Australia, the greatest challenge for us all is the rapid development of secularism that downplays the importance of spiritual awareness and faith. We pray that the next generation of resources will enable us to engage the whole community more fully and find ways to enrich the lives of those within and beyond the Church.

Revd Dr Ian Price
The Upper Room Australian Editor and CEO, MediaCom Education

The Editor writes...

One of our favourite holiday destinations, which my husband and I love to visit, is Dartmouth in Devon, where the River Dart meets the sea and where the riverfront is crowded with boats. Among the smallest are the Castle Ferry boats, which take people to and from Dartmouth Castle, guarding the entrance to the river mouth. It is only a ten-minute trip, yet one of the best ways to see this lovely river port. One of the ferry boats teaches me a lesson every time we visit, because its name is 'Y-Worry'.

Many of us are prone to worry. It is a natural reaction to situations that trouble us now or which might arise in the future. We worry about our jobs, whether we will be made redundant; we worry about our family members, be they young or old; we worry about our health as we wait for test results. And yet, deep down, we know that worry is a corrosive habit that does nothing to help a situation; in fact, it makes everything more difficult. At worst, unchecked worry can lead to acute anxiety, and we feel powerless to think or act rationally.

Jesus offers us the perfect antidote to worry. In Matthew 6:25–34 he compares our lives to those of the birds and the flowers, all of which flourish without worrying about food or appearance for today or tomorrow. God supplies their needs, says Jesus, and do you not realise that you are of more value to God than they? 'Can any one of you by worrying add a single hour to your life?' he asks (v. 27, NIV). We know we cannot.

The one thing we can do with worry is to hand it over to God. Of course there are events in life which we find hard to cope with and which frighten us, but given over in faith to God, we will find that the most overwhelming difficulty can be faced. Instead of struggling with worry by ourselves, we can remember, 'The eternal God is your refuge, and underneath are the everlasting arms' (Deuteronomy 33:27, NIV).

Susan Hibbins
Editor of the UK edition

The Bible readings are selected with great care, and we urge you to include the suggested reading in your devotional time.

Adopted

Read Galatians 4:1–7

You received a Spirit that shows you are adopted as his children. With this Spirit we cry, 'Abba, Father.'
Romans 8:15 (CEB)

As part of a Bible lesson, I gave each child a folded slip of paper with a word written on it, indicating how God sees him or her: 'loved', 'redeemed', 'forgiven', 'valued' and 'precious', to name a few. As each word was read aloud, the children smiled and occasionally cheered. But the child who received the word 'adopted' was disappointed. 'Why did you give me this word?' he asked. 'I'd rather have one of the others.' For him, adoption had a negative connotation. But I thought 'adoption' was the best word because it embodied all the others.

Adoption is a conscious choice to make someone part of a family. It creates a new relationship that entitles the adopted person to all the rights and privileges that belong to a biological child. As believers, we have been adopted into God's family. God is our parent who protects, loves, forgives and accepts us. We now carry the family name and will eventually take up residence in God's house.

From God's perspective, adoption means that we are chosen, accepted, valued and loved without reservation.

Prayer: *Dear Lord, thank you for loving us enough to make us a permanent part of your family. Amen*

Thought for the day: God has chosen me.

Esther L. Bonner (California, US)

PRAYER FOCUS: FAMILIES WAITING TO ADOPT

Good Soil

Read Luke 8:4–8
'Other seed fell on rock. As it grew, it dried up because it had no moisture.'
Luke 8:6 (CEB)

As I prepared the soil for spring planting, the parable of the sower came to mind. I remembered times when I had tried to plant a garden in hard, rocky soil. Few seeds were able to survive and grow. I needed to bring in compost and sand to mix into the soil. Each year, I have found areas of the garden that have become depleted, needing to be enriched.

Jesus used the parable in today's reading to help the disciples understand that not everyone would accept their teachings. The soil of some listeners' hearts was in no condition for seeds to grow and thrive. By the same token, our hearts are not always good soil. We can never assume they are rich and fertile. Life's experiences can help prepare our hearts to grow and mature, to become the soil God needs for planting the seeds. But we also need ongoing prayer, Bible study and Christian fellowship to keep our hearts rich and fertile.

The pleasure I receive as I watch my garden thrive pales when compared to the pleasure God receives as the kingdom grows and blossoms.

Prayer: *Dear Lord, prepare our hearts for the planting of your word. Amen*

Thought for the day: God's word can enrich my heart.

Madeline Peterson (Nebraska, US)

Not Alone

Read James 5:13–15
Trust in him at all times, you people; pour out your hearts to him, for God is our refuge.
Psalm 62:8 (NIV)

The day was going fine until I got to the hospital for a routine appointment with my cardiologist. When he had finished the cardiac catheterisation procedure, he spoke frankly: 'You need open-heart surgery.' No words had ever crushed me so much—not even at Christmas time when, at the age of 22, I was told that I would be deployed to Vietnam. I was not even so shocked when, on Mothering Sunday at the age of 55, I received my orders for a tour of duty in Iraq.

Many thoughts raced through my mind as my wife tried to console me. I remained stunned and overwhelmed. In that fleeting moment, any semblance of faith seemed to vanish.

However, I soon rallied when I received many calls of support from friends, family and church members. And their prayers did not fail. I realised that I was not alone! I remembered Psalm 46:1: 'God is our refuge and strength, an ever present help in trouble.' This scripture revived my faith in my Saviour. He has always comforted me in time of need. I learned not to doubt the power of my Lord—no matter what the circumstances.

Prayer: *Merciful God, restore our faith when we are overcome by challenging circumstances. Amen*

Thought for the day: The prayers of my community can give me strength.

Santos Vega (Puerto Rico)

Daily Rituals

Read John 17:20–24

'I desire faithful love and not sacrifice, the knowledge of God instead of entirely burned offerings.'
Hosea 6:6 (CEB)

There's something about tea that I find comforting. It isn't just the flavour but the process of preparing it as well. Warm the pot, steep the leaves, pour the tea into my cup and add milk and a little sugar; then take a sip and feel my tensions ease.

Going through this ritual helps me wake up in the morning, clear my head when I'm overwhelmed, and relax at day's end. Focusing on each step draws my attention to the task at hand.

What would be the point of brewing a cup of tea if we didn't take the time to enjoy it at the end? But sometimes, we do that in our spiritual lives. We sing the hymn, read the verse or pray the prayer without actually engaging with God. Rituals and disciplines are meant to lead us into intimacy with God. Simply going through the motions of faith will not satisfy our thirst for him.

Making a cup of tea and savouring the experience is a model for practising spiritual disciplines. Each day we can turn simple actions into times of intentional connection with God. As we go through the day, we may say a prayer, sing a song, give an offering or read scripture. With each step we work our way toward the desired outcome: a closer relationship with God.

Prayer: *Dear God, help us to make time each day to steep in your love for us and to pour out that love to others. Amen*

Thought for the day: What rituals do I find helpful in moving me closer to God?

Megan L. Anderson (Indiana, US)

With Us Always

Read Matthew 6:25–34

[Jesus] got up, rebuked the wind and said to the waves, 'Quiet! Be still!' Then the wind died down and it was completely calm.
Mark 4:39 (NIV)

I was having a rough morning. I hadn't slept well, and I was worried. Family members were struggling with health issues. A valued employee had resigned. I was trying to meet work deadlines. As I stood making small talk during the coffee hour at church, my mind was filled with anxiety.

A friend walked up to me. 'That is the most beautiful cross I have ever seen!' she said and pointed to a wooden cross that hung in the coffee area. The church caretaker had made it from two gnarled tree limbs, lashed together with cord. I told her it had been there for several years. She put her hands to her face and said, 'Isn't that amazing? That beautiful cross has been there all this time, and I hadn't even noticed.'

I studied the cross—the symbol of God's sacrificial love for us. It seemed to reach out to me in my time of distress. On that morning, the cross and the comment from my friend brought me a message from God: 'I am here for you. I have always been here with you.'

When we get caught up in worry, we can look around for signs of God's presence. When we turn our worries over to God through prayer, we can receive his comfort.

Prayer: *Dear Lord, thank you for guiding us through the storms of life. Open our eyes that we might see the signs of your presence. Amen*

Thought for the day: I will be attentive to signs of God's presence.

David McCain (Louisiana, US)

Generation to Generation

Read Hebrews 13:1–3, 15–16
[Paul said,] 'In everything I did, I showed you that by this kind of hard work we must help the weak, remembering the words the Lord Jesus himself said: "It is more blessed to give than to receive." '
Acts 20:35 (NIV)

As a little girl I enjoyed watching my mother prepare hearty stews, and bake golden loaves of bread and rich, velvety cakes and pastries. Close to supper time she would pack portions of this food into a basket to take to a neighbour in need.

One day on our way home, I asked Mum why we had to give the food away. She replied, 'Always remember that it makes God happy when we share, and that it is more blessed to give than to receive.' These words became indelibly etched in my mind and on my heart.

Recently I enjoyed a visit with my eight-year-old granddaughter. We sat on the patio, which was covered with acorns from the oak tree above. She told me her class were planning a mission project to help those in need and that they had to earn money to donate to the project. I offered her a job cleaning acorns off the patio. As she worked, she told me that her goal in life was to become successful in business and give half of her earnings to those in need. I said, 'It makes God happy when we share, and it is more blessed to give than to receive.' She looked up and softly said, 'I know.'

The words my mother spoke to me will continue to be shared for generations to come.

Prayer: *Thank you, God, for parents who lead by faithful example and for granting us opportunities to pass wisdom on to the children in our lives. Amen*

Thought for the day: With whom will I share God's blessings today?

Florence Anne Apperson (Virginia, US)

Old Fish, New Fish

Read Matthew 22:34–40

'You must love the Lord your God with all your heart, with all your being, and with all your mind… You must love your neighbour as you love yourself.'
Matthew 22:37, 39 (CEB)

Well over 100,000 miles ago I had a new car and put one of those shiny fish on the back to let everyone know, 'I am a Christian!' As the car and I both aged, I came to the realisation that motoring around with a fish on the back of my car set me up for scrutiny. I had to ask, 'What do others really see when they look at me? Do they see an example of a Christ-like life? Or do they see a hypocrite?' After all, I do not always love others as I should, and I know I frequently fail to keep my tongue under control. Like Paul, instead of doing what I know is right, I sometimes do the things I hate (see Romans 7:15).

A few years back, a hailstorm did some obvious damage to both the car and the fish. No windows were broken, but the car sustained many dents. The hail also broke off part of the fish's tail and scoured away most of the shiny finish. Somehow, I am much more comfortable with the less-than-perfect fish. Every time I load or unload something from the boot of the car, I am reminded that while I am less than the shining example I strive to be, I will continue to strive. That is the Christian's walk.

Prayer: *Dear Father, forgive us when we miss the mark, and help us to live our faith in a way that leads others to you. Amen*

Thought for the day: What do my actions show others about Christ?

Cindy Love (Texas, US)

Things Above

Read Colossians 3:1–4

I have calmed and quieted my soul, like a weaned child with its mother.
Psalm 131:2 (NRSV)

I often ride my motorbike in the middle of traffic in Marseille, one of the most congested cities in France. Surrounded by all the potentially dangerous cars, exhaust fumes, engine noises, sirens and sweltering heat, I sometimes feel as if I might be in hell.

In these moments, I like to obey the exhortation of the Apostle Paul in Colossians 3:2; 'Set your minds on things above, not on earthly things.' I love to imagine Jesus approaching. He hugs me and gathers me into his arms. I am totally loved, fully accepted and forgiven, completely holy, peaceful and serene. I am God's child.

Setting my mind on these things helps me to go through tough times. And this is not simply the fruit of my imagination. It is reality! We are all God's children, held in God's arms, and deeply loved.

Paul encourages us to focus on this reality, and we can do it every day. We can take a moment and set our minds on the reality that is above.

Prayer: *Dear Lord, help us to set our minds on the truth of your love for us every day and at all times. Amen*

Thought for the day: At any time, I can set my mind on things above.

Daniel Sebbah (France)

The Stones will Cry Out

Read Luke 19:32–40

'I tell you,' [Jesus] replied, 'if they keep quiet, the stones will cry out.'
Luke 19:40 (NIV)

Last year just before Easter our minister preached a beautiful sermon on today's reading about Jesus' triumphal entry into Jerusalem. The pastor spoke about how important it is for each of us not only to live a Christian life but to proclaim and share our faith with others. As we left, the stewards gave everyone a small stone as a reminder of Jesus' words: 'if they keep quiet, the stones will cry out'.

I carry that stone with me almost every day. Whenever I reach into my pocket for my car keys or change and touch the stone, I am reminded of God's love for me. At that moment, I usually say a prayer of thanksgiving.

In this day of impersonal contact with mobile phones and social media, I think of what a blessing it is to be able to pray and know that God loves us and is listening to our concerns regardless of our circumstances. It is also a blessing to be able to share that love with others.

Prayer: *Dear Father, thank you for sending your Son to show us how to live loving and fulfilling lives. We pray as Jesus taught us, saying, 'Our Father in heaven, hallowed be your name, your kingdom come, your will be done, on earth as it is in heaven. Give us today our daily bread. And forgive us our debts, as we also have forgiven our debtors. And lead us not into temptation, but deliver us from the evil one.'* Amen*

Thought for the day: How can I share my faith today?

P. Ross Ramsay (North Carolina, US)

* Matthew 6:9–13 (NIV)

Following

Read Luke 5:1–11

When Jesus spoke again to the people, he said, 'I am the light of the world. Whoever follows me will never walk in darkness, but will have the light of life.'
John 8:12 (NIV)

The youth group travelled in convoy. They thought that the people in the first car knew their destination, and the first car continued to lead the way through the neighbourhood. When they had gone round in circles several times, one of the young people phoned someone in the first car to ask if they knew where they were going. The people in the first car answered that they didn't, but because everyone was following, they thought they must be headed in the right direction.

We tend to think that if many people are following someone, that person must be the right person to follow. We don't always check to see whether that person will lead us in the right direction.

But we can be sure in following our Lord Jesus Christ. He said, 'I am the light of the world. Whoever follows me will never walk in darkness, but will have the light of life' (John 8:12). He told Simon Peter, James and John to follow. 'So they pulled their boats up on shore, left everything and followed him' (Luke 5:11). Only Jesus can lead us to the ultimate destination and give us life.

Prayer: *Lord Jesus, we praise you for your amazing grace. Help us to follow you each step of our lives. Amen*

Thought for the day: How will I follow Christ today?

Tracy Jensen (California, US)

Give Me the Words, Lord

Read Psalm 46:1–11

'When they arrest you, do not worry about what to say or how to say it. At that time you will be given what to say, for it will not be you speaking, but the Spirit of your Father speaking through you.'
Matthew 10:19–20 (NIV)

After the attacks in the USA on 11 September 2001, I was asked to help at the New York City Family Assistance Center. I was assigned to the legal division to assist with benefits for the victims' families.

I had been happy to help when asked, but this assignment filled me with apprehension. What could I possibly say when faced with families who had lost someone close to them so violently and so suddenly? Words failed me completely. I felt inadequate to do what I was being asked to do.

In my church we had been praying the Psalms, especially Psalm 46. So I turned to the Psalms to find peace. Instead, my Bible fell open to a passage from Matthew where Jesus instructed his disciples before sending them out on a mission. He told them that it would not be they who would be speaking but the Spirit of God speaking through them. I continued reading and meditating on this passage throughout my months working at the Center to remind me that God would give me the words I needed to speak to his people.

Whether through the Bible, others with whom I share my faith journey or the world around me, God is still speaking to me. I want to be sure to listen.

Prayer: *O God, as we find ourselves overwhelmed by the clamour of a needy world, quiet every voice but yours, so we will be able to know your peace and share it with others. Amen*

Thought for the day: God is still speaking. Today I will be quiet and listen.

Mary Tufts (New York, US)

PRAYER FOCUS: FAMILIES AFFECTED BY VIOLENCE

Begin with Truth

Read Lamentations 3:25–33

Whatever is true, whatever is honourable, whatever is just, whatever is pure, whatever is pleasing, whatever is commendable, if there is any excellence and if there is anything worthy of praise, think about these things.

Philippians 4:8 (NRSV)

Although I am generally an optimist, I know things don't always turn out well. Financial fears sometimes come true. Biopsy results sometimes show cancer. People disappoint us. Problems arise.

I was often confused by Paul's instruction in the verse quoted above. He asks us to dwell upon all those positive qualities.

This was brought home to me shortly after a church meeting in which a number of problems were discussed. I don't want to go to church—not even church meetings—to hear about problems. Church is a place I go to be reminded of God's love and to be encouraged.

But the morning after that meeting, I happened across this passage from Philippians. And for the first time I noticed that Paul starts his list with whatsoever things are true. He doesn't gloss over life's realities; he begins with them. If things are truly bad we need to deal with them. Best of all, the same God who blesses us is here to help us right the wrongs, solve the problems and weather the storms that this life invariably brings.

Prayer: *Dear Lord, help us to appreciate the blessings and deal with the realities that come to us today. Amen*

Thought for the day: Whatever life brings, God is here to help me through it.

Bruce Bedingfield (Illinois, US)

A Spiritual Family

Read Ecclesiastes 3:1–8

There's a season for everything and a time for every matter under the heavens... a time for planting and a time for uprooting what was planted.
Ecclesiastes 3:1–2 (CEB)

It was my 47th birthday. I was celebrating it without my family that year because God had called me to serve in a new church in a different area of the country from where they all lived.

My morning's Bible reading was the one above; it reminded me that not only had I been uprooted from my comfort zone, but I had been planted into a new church family. And this family had sent me a birthday card and many text messages that made me feel less alone. This church family had been joining me in praising God that I was among them, where God wanted me to be on my birthday.

As the day drew to a close, I realised that I had much to be thankful for. Although I knew that the coming year would not be easy in some ways, I also knew that God had prepared me by reminding me that life has seasons of planting and seasons of uprooting and that none of them are outside his magnificent sovereignty and grace.

Prayer: *Loving God, thank you for making brothers and sisters out of complete strangers and for giving us a spiritual family wherever we may go. Amen*

Thought for the day: Who are my spiritual family?

Carol Denereaz (New South Wales, Australia)

A Concert of God's Word

Read Psalm 100

Make a joyful noise to the Lord, all the earth.
Psalm 100:1 (NRSV)

When I was a little girl, I had piano lessons. Playing the piano was not something that came naturally to me and my teacher assigned me only the simplest of tunes. Within a year or two, I stopped having lessons. Several years later, I picked up my old piano books and began to play the familiar melodies. For whatever reason, this time I was interested in learning to play and practised daily. I progressed to playing more advanced pieces and eventually had many pieces memorised. Although in the beginning I stumbled and hesitated, over time the music found its way into my heart. Once, while on holiday, I even performed an impromptu concert for the guests of the hotel where I was staying.

Decades later, I am going through the same procedure trying to memorise scripture. I initially stumble my way through, then at some point the scripture moves from my head to my heart. As I speak the verses, the words come pouring out of my mouth with even more joy, enthusiasm and love than those songs I played long ago on the piano. Alas, I have long since given up the piano, but God's word is something I'll never give up. Who knows when I might be called upon to perform an impromptu concert?

Prayer: *Loving God, thank you for your gift of music and for the truth of your everlasting word. In Jesus' name we pray. Amen*

Thought for the day: When we keep scripture in our hearts, we are never far from God.

Amy Hayes Burling (Florida, US)

A Sympathetic Saviour

Read Hebrews 2:10–18

Because he himself suffered when he was tempted, he is able to help those who are being tempted.

Hebrews 2:18 (NIV)

Someone in my Bible study group remarked that Jesus experienced all the same temptations and trials that we face today. Then one member's head shot up, and with a questioning look in her eyes she said, 'You mean Jesus went through puberty?' Although the Bible clearly tells us that Jesus was tempted as we are, we still tend to overlook his humanity. Somehow we think he was above all the nitty-gritty of daily life.

Jesus came as a helpless baby, needing someone to supply his every need. He grew up in the home of a carpenter, so he probably endured his fair share of childhood cuts, bumps and bruises along with daily dust and dirt. And he also braved puberty with all its ups and downs. Although Jesus experienced life in a different time and culture, the risen Christ understands and identifies with our daily dilemmas.

Whenever we feel alone and wonder who will understand or how we can continue, we can remember that Jesus has already been there. He hears our cries and stands ready to walk with us through whatever difficulties we face. He holds us up in our lowest moments. He offers hope when life seems hopeless. He celebrates with us when our hardships cease.

Prayer: *O God, thank you for your never-failing presence in every circumstance. Amen*

Thought for the day: Jesus knows. Jesus cares.

Diana C. Derringer (Kentucky, US)

Not the Final Word

Read John 11:38–44
Jesus called in a loud voice, 'Lazarus, come out!'
John 11:43 (NIV)

On a trip to Israel, I visited the gravesite that many people think is Lazarus' tomb. It was a sombre but hopeful experience. Being in that place brought to my mind the death of my own brother years before. I recalled the feeling of disbelief as my father announced to our family that our brother had been killed. There was a sense of numbness, emptiness—a sense of 'now what?' As I listened to what my father said and saw my parents' grief, I felt helpless and out of control. As I stood in silence at Lazarus' tomb, death was very real to me.

Then, suddenly, my melancholy memories at Lazarus' tomb were broken by the voice of someone reading the story of Jesus' raising his friend from death. In that moment, I felt what Mary and Martha must have felt when they saw their brother emerge from the darkness of the tomb: unspeakable joy, as if the world were in order again.

I was reminded that death is not the final word—only a comma, a pause, a pathway to a greater life with the One who gives life and is Life. In times of grief and loss, those who faithfully follow Christ can hold on to joyful hope.

Prayer: *Life-giving Lord, thank you for giving us hope even when we are facing death. We joyfully receive your gift of abundant life. Amen*

Thought for the day: Resurrection gives hope in the face of death.

Dyton L. Owen (Nebraska, US)

Hide-and-Seek

Read Psalm 31:1–5

The name of the Lord is a strong tower; the righteous run into it and are safe.

Proverbs 18:10 (NRSV)

Hide-and-seek was one of my favourite childhood games. I remember curling up behind my dad's armchair, stifling a giggle that threatened to erupt. My sister would prowl through the house chanting my name, anxious to spot a rogue foot or hand that would expose my hiding place. Most of the time, I couldn't keep quiet long enough to avoid discovery. But every now and then, she passed me by. Within seconds, I would bolt from my cover and whisk toward 'home base', the game's safe harbour. Sheer exhilaration and relief flooded my seven-year-old body every time I escaped my sister's stalking and made it to the game's sanctuary, singing out, 'I'm safe, I'm safe!'

I'm not a small child any more, but sometimes life feels like a game of hide-and-seek. Jobs, relationships, parenting, heartaches, medical issues, addictions—life's difficulties tempt us to take cover and to retreat from the pain. But scripture gives us a map to 'home base', which offers refuge and protection the world cannot provide. 'The name of the Lord is a strong tower' (Proverbs 18:10), our safe place, our destination when we are tired of running and hiding. God offers relief for the righteous who seek security in the strength of his presence.

Prayer: *Dear God, help us to recognise your power and to seek you during times of trouble, pain, joy and gladness. Amen*

Thought for the day: When I face a problem, I can find refuge in God.

Briana M. Combs (Kentucky, US)

Privileged to Teach

Read Mark 10:13–16

All that heard him were astonished at his understanding and answers.
Luke 2:47 (KJV)

I recently turned 80 years old. Even at this age, I cannot forget my Sunday school teachers. I attended Sunday school from the age of three until I was 18. It was during this period that I received Jesus as my Saviour. I am grateful for my teachers who taught the living word of God with deep commitment and love. All these years later, I still have great respect for my Sunday school teachers.

In Luke 2, we see twelve-year-old Jesus arguing with the Jewish priests in the temple, and they were all astonished by his wisdom and answers. He was well-versed in scripture.

What about our children? I firmly believe God has a plan to use Sunday school to produce faithful servants for the Church.

Children are precious in the sight of God, and it was my privilege to serve as a Sunday school teacher for about three decades. By attending Sunday school our children can learn about Jesus Christ and the scriptures, and we can pass on the lessons of faith to future generations.

Prayer: *God of truth, bless Sunday school teachers and students and make them fruitful for the Church. In Jesus' name we pray. Amen*

Thought for the day: How can I support my congregation's Sunday school ministry?

Jayant Samuel Trajker (Gujarat, India)

The Anchor and the Cross

Read Hebrews 6:13–20

We have this hope as an anchor for the soul, firm and secure.
Hebrews 6:19 (NIV)

Our grandson Landon loves boats. When he visits, he pretends our long front porch is a ship. He 'hoists the sails' by tugging on the cords of the window blinds and 'swabs the deck' with a dust mop. Outside, the garden hose becomes a rope to haul up the anchor.

One morning as we strolled through the neighbourhood, Landon spotted a bronze plaque fastened to a rock in the centre of a garden. 'An anchor!' he shouted. 'An anchor!'

I tugged him away from the garden. 'That's not an anchor, that's a cross.' 'It's an anchor!' His voice was loud and insistent.

Later that day, as I thought about the event, I chuckled at his conviction that the cross was an anchor. Then the words of a familiar hymn filtered through my mind: 'We have an anchor that keeps the soul, steadfast and sure while the billows roll, fastened to the Rock which cannot move, grounded firm and deep in the Saviour's love' (Priscilla J. Owens, 1882).

It turns out that we were both right. The assurance of salvation represented by the cross is anchored by Christ's divine provision. His sacrifice provides us with a secure anchor of hope.

Prayer: *Heavenly Father, so many things in life point to your steadfast presence. Help us attune to the everyday experiences that direct us to you. Amen*

Thought for the day: The cross is an anchor for all who believe.

Judyann Grant (New York, US)

Serving Others

Read John 13:3–5

[Jesus said] 'Now that I, your Lord and Teacher, have washed your feet, you also should wash one another's feet.'

John 13:14 (NIV)

Years ago in London, among the homeless people in the city, there was a little old woman known as 'the sock lady'. She travelled round to the different places where the homeless congregated at night, wiping their sore, tired feet and giving them clean, warm socks. If you have ever walked for hours on city streets then you will know how tired your feet feel by the end of the day. So we can all understand how grateful the homeless people were to 'the sock lady'.

Jesus left us an example of serving others by washing his disciples' feet. Usually this was a task for a servant, but here Jesus, the Teacher, deliberately takes on the task, not just as an act of love but also to teach his disciples an important lesson. The leader of all is firstly the servant of all.

Prayer: *Loving Lord, teach us to serve others, as you, our Lord and Teacher, did. Amen*

Thought for the day: Today I will look for opportunities to serve others.

Ann Phillips (Somerset, England)

Keeping a Connection

Read John 15:1–11

Devote yourselves to prayer, being watchful and thankful.
Colossians 4:2 (NIV)

We enjoy entertaining our friend who is a Chinese exchange student. He's enthusiastic about his classes and his time with our American family. However, each evening at 7.30 pm he excuses himself, regardless of where he is and what's going on. Why? He always calls his family in Beijing at 8.00 pm. There his family gather around the phone, waiting to hear about his adventures that day. Nothing prevents him from keeping this appointment.

We admire his dedication and love for his family, and we wonder if we're that faithful when it comes to our commitment to God through prayer. Do we let interruptions and a busy schedule keep us from our most important communication each day?

This young man's relationship with his family has made us more aware of the tremendous privilege and opportunity of prayer. We can pray any time, anywhere and about anything. It's amazing that God, who created everything, loves us and wants a relationship with us. We can have the same dedication to God as our exchange student has to his family. I want to hold this thought in my heart: 'God, I can't wait to talk to you.'

Prayer: *Thank you, dear God, for the power and privilege of prayer. We need your love as well as your wisdom and guidance daily. Help us to spend more time with you. Amen*

Thought for the day: Our prayer time with God is too important to miss.

Donna J. Eliason (Washington, US)

Seeds of the Gospel

Read 2 Corinthians 9:6–15

He who supplies seed to the sower and bread for food will also supply and increase your store of seed and will enlarge the harvest of your righteousness.

2 Corinthians 9:10 (NIV)

The soil was tilled and the seeds carefully planted. The spring rains were timely, and with proper care our garden flourished. We bottled 50 jars of green beans and were able to give away large numbers of beans to others. When the yield slowed and the weeds started to thrive, I decided to till the ground, turning under what remained. More good rains followed, and in about two weeks volunteer beans began to grow where the tilling process had planted mature seeds. Now, though it is past the normal season for beans, we are able again to share this bountiful crop with others.

The Bible has many teachings on bearing fruit as witnesses for God wherever we are. Jesus used parables about nature or daily life to teach spiritual truth. In Matthew 13, he describes the one who receives seed on the good ground as someone who hears and accepts the word and bears fruit, even a hundredfold. Just as God provided the bountiful crop in the prepared garden in the parable, he will help us to grow and mature and become fruitful witnesses to the kingdom. Jesus reminds us that we did not choose him, but he chose us to go and bear fruit that will last (see John 15:16). Then we are able to share this fruit with others.

Prayer: *Lord of heaven, help us to be bold, wise and faithful in our witness. Amen*

Thought for the day: Am I prepared to bear fruit as a witness for God?

Walter N. Maris (Missouri, US)

God's Constant Presence

Read Jeremiah 18:1–6

You, O Lord, are our Father. We are the clay, you are the potter; we are all the work of your hand.
Isaiah 64:8 (NIV)

I sat on the beach, enjoying the fresh breeze, the sound of the waves and the smell of the sea. I watched a small boy with his father; the child was building a sand castle, but he was using soft, dry sand that collapsed easily. He looked to his father, who showed him how to dig for firmer, damp sand. The work progressed, but then the bucketful of sand was too heavy for the child to lift; he need his father to help. The father was unfailingly patient as sand was knocked down or blown over. The child laughed and struggled, confidently looking to his father for help.

I thought of the way our heavenly Father patiently guides us through our difficulties, moulding and shaping us in his image. The more we look to him for guidance, the more confident we become in the knowledge of his constant presence so that we can accomplish even difficult things with his unfailing support.

Prayer: *Father, we thank you for your constant guidance, for your patience that never ends, and that we can always turn to you for help. Amen*

Thought for the day: God is with us in the everyday circumstances of our lives.

Kathleen Sharps (Cheshire, England)

Riptides

Read Romans 10:12–15

[Jesus commanded], 'Go into all the world and preach the gospel to all creation.'
Mark 16:15 (NIV)

From the road above Ipanema Beach near Rio de Janeiro, Brazil, I saw a terrible sight. A young man was caught in a fierce riptide and quickly swept out to sea. He swam toward shore with all his might but only exhausted himself. He went under, came up screaming and waving for help, went under, and was never seen again.

I know how to deal with riptides. If only I could have spent a few minutes with that young man before he went into the sea, to explain what to do if caught in a riptide! I might have made him feel uncomfortable or he might have rejected my explanation, or he might not have wanted to listen. But still, if he had heard my few simple instructions, he would have known how to survive.

Something similar applies to the good news of salvation in Christ. With a simple explanation about believing in God's sacrifice of Jesus and in the power of Jesus' resurrection, people can be rescued when they become caught in the 'riptides' of life—divorce, the death of loved ones, financial disaster or broken health. When we share our hope in Christ, some people might feel uncomfortable, reject us or consider themselves too busy to discuss salvation. Still, the gospel truths we share with them can encourage them during the trials of life and give them hope for eternity.

Prayer: *Dear Lord, help us to be bold in proclaiming your gospel. Amen*

Thought for the day: With whom can I share my hope in Christ today?

Randy Swanson (Utah, US)

Focusing on the Divine

Read Acts 17:24–27

Are not two sparrows sold for a penny? Yet not one of them will fall to the ground outside your Father's care.
Matthew 10:29 (NIV)

That Sunday the pews were filled. I was seated near the front surveying the gathered church family when suddenly a tiny spider came dangling down from the ceiling before my eyes. My first impulse was to smash the unwelcome guest to the floor, but then I stopped and began to ponder with wonder this tiny creature spinning its web from such lofty heights.

Later, reflecting upon my experience that Sunday morning, I remembered the Bible passage about God's concern over a sparrow that falls. I realised that God created that tiny spider, and I was filled with a sense of awe.

God moves in mysterious ways that are sometimes easy to miss. On that day, my encounter with the spider reminded me to focus on God's presence in that place and in my life.

Prayer: *Dear God, help us to be more aware of your presence in all that you have created. We pray in the name of Jesus, who taught us to pray, 'Father, hallowed be your name, your kingdom come. Give us each day our daily bread. Forgive us our sins, for we also forgive everyone who sins against us. And lead us not into temptation.'* Amen*

Thought for the day: God is closer than we think.

Bill Kidwell (Ohio, US)

PRAYER FOCUS: GRATITUDE FOR THE BEAUTY OF CREATION
* Luke 11:2–4 (NIV)

Desire to Change

Read Hebrews 12:7–11

Discipline always seems painful rather than pleasant at the time, but later it yields the peaceful fruit of righteousness to those who have been trained by it.

Hebrews 12:11 (NRSV)

'I really said that?' The new teacher's assistant was unaware that she had just spent five minutes berating a struggling student.

Hearing her words and irritated tone of voice, the demoralised boy had slumped in his chair. As her supervisor, I wanted to help her understand the damage her words had caused. She insisted, through tears, that she did not realise she had spoken in that way. Her sorrow indicated a desire to change, so I showed her other ways to handle frustration in the classroom. She relaxed and began to enjoy her time with the student. He began to engage again.

In my relationship with God I find myself doing the same thing. 'I did that, God?' My disbelief has been equally genuine and pain-filled when God has helped me to see my shortcomings. In Revelation 3:19, God says, 'I reprove and discipline those whom I love.' How often do we gossip and not think about how hurtful it is? How often do we disagree with someone and assume that they are in the wrong? How often do we fail to tell the whole truth?

We may not recognise our sins until God points them out. When we respond to correction, God, without condemnation, gives us strength and courage to change.

Prayer: *Dear God, give us the willingness to recognise our sinful behaviour and to accept your help to change our ways. Thank you for always forgiving us. Amen*

Thought for the day: What change is God urging me to make in my life today?

Karen Dorsey (Oregon, US)

Where to Focus?

Read Psalm 145:3–7

Do not conform to the pattern of this world, but be transformed by the renewing of your mind. Then you will be able to test and approve what God's will is.
Romans 12:2 (NIV)

I looked up to see cobwebs outside on my upstairs window. As I thought about the best way to clean them up, along came a wagtail that flew to the ledge and sang me a pretty song.

This experience reminded me of the way God comes into our messy lives. When I concentrated on the bird and his song, I forgot the cobwebs. In a similar way, focusing on praising God tends to put my problems into perspective—helping them to fade into the background. If we open our eyes and look around, we will find God always at work bringing joy, light and a song into the difficult places.

I hope that, with the power of God at work within me, I too am able to bring a song into the lives of those whom my life touches. Maybe our actions, attitudes and how we speak to others will brush away some cobwebs and bring joy. As we are open to the leading of the Holy Spirit and as we renew our minds with God's word, we are transformed. Then we can also transform the world around us.

Prayer: *Loving Father, we thank you for your beautiful creation and praise you for the way you love us and care for us. Amen*

Thought for the day: I can put my problems into perspective when I focus on praising God.

Ann Stewart (South Australia, Australia)

It's Not Fair!

Read Matthew 20:1–16

In [Christ] we have redemption through his blood, the forgiveness of sins, in accordance with the riches of God's grace that he lavished on us.
Ephesians 1:7–8 (NIV)

'It's not fair!' As a father of five, I have heard that a few times. I don't think we ever grow out of that feeling. Jesus told a parable about fairness. At the end of the workday, the landowner paid the same wage to all the workers—the ones who worked one hour and the ones who had worked all day. That's doesn't seem fair. The twelve-hour workers were not happy. Why should the one-hour workers get paid as much as they? They were even angry with the land-owner!

That's not fair—unless I'm the one who began work at 5.00 in the afternoon. If I'm the 5.00 pm worker, I'm probably not too concerned about what's fair; I just appreciate this gift of grace.

Maybe I've been standing all day waiting to be chosen for work, only to be passed over—again. Maybe I was feeling unworthy, unwanted—rejected time and time again. Watching other people be chosen may have made me want to give up and go home.

But we are all the 5.00 pm workers. We've been chosen and called to work by none other than God! The Creator of heaven and earth has called us to work for his kingdom and to share in the riches of his grace—not because we deserve it, but because we don't. That's not fair; that's grace.

Prayer: *Gracious God, thank you for the grace you offer us and each of your children. Forgive us when we resent your gracious love for others. Amen*

Thought for the day: God generously offers grace to everyone.

Michael Vaughn (Tennessee, US)

The Lord's Song

Read Zephaniah 3:14–20

The Lord, your God, is in your midst, a warrior who gives victory; he will rejoice over you with gladness, he will renew you in his love; he will exult over you with loud singing.

Zephaniah 3:17 (NRSV)

When I was eight years old, I asked the Lord into my heart at Sunday school and soon discovered the joy of singing and dancing for Jesus. At school, when the other children bullied me, I was mocked, laughed at and made fun of. I often cried all the way home. To comfort myself, I listened to classical records in the garage and swirled to the loud music. I sang simple praises to Jesus: 'I love you, Lord', 'Praise you, Lord' and 'I lift my hands up, Lord.'

Again, I found victory in song and dance when my children were born. I struggled with new motherhood, but the Lord helped me. I sang with my babies, and I danced with them in my arms. Their gentle, soothing responses brought me great joy. When I found the Zephaniah verse above, I realised that my singing and dancing simply gave back what the Lord had already expressed to me.

Years later, I still find that joy. I marvel that the Creator of the universe shows me love and 'rejoices and sings over me'. The Lord rejoices over each of us. Our life of praise gives back the love God has given us.

Prayer: *O Lord, thank you for your song of love. Help us to sing your love to those who haven't yet heard your song. Amen*

Thought for the day: The Lord rejoices over me!

Pamela J. Caldwell (California, US)

Shining God's Goodness

Read Matthew 5:13-16

Let your light shine before others, so that they may see your good works and give glory to your Father in heaven.
Matthew 5:16 (NRSV)

Sometimes we see the evil in this world and wonder how a loving God could let it go unchecked. I think perhaps we should be asking a different question. Aren't goodness, love and care evidence of the presence of God in our midst?

I experienced God's goodness first-hand when recovering from knee-replacement surgery in a physiotherapy clinic. My recovery team and the staff members I met were from Russia, India, the Philippines, Albania and Romania. These carers from all over the world were like ministers to me. They all had one purpose in mind: to provide for my recovery needs with compassion. I experienced God's presence in every caring act.

There may be much evil in the world, but the goodness of God shines through it all when people show love and compassion to one another. God is love (see 1 John 4:8). When we act compassionately, we reveal him to the world.

Prayer: *Loving Creator, thank you for being present to us when we look for you. Help us live a life to show your glory. Amen*

Thought for the day: How can I show God's goodness and love to someone today?

Stanley L. Hayes (Michigan, US)

Stealing Jesus

Read Psalm 119:1–8

Happy are those who keep his decrees, who seek him with their whole heart.
Psalm 119:2 (NRSV)

I could tell something was wrong with my friend before she made it to my cell. She had a bewildered look on her face as she approached me. 'You will never guess what someone did to me,' she said. I encouraged her to tell me what had happened.

A Christian inspirational book had been stolen from her bunk. My friend was upset because she had been inspired by the readings and had taken to reading the book as a daily devotional guide. As someone who tries to see the glass half full in life, I lightheartedly asked her, 'You mean someone stole Jesus off your bed?' My question made her chuckle. She said, 'I suppose you could say that.'

I am not one to advocate stealing, especially in prison. But I hope that if someone steals Jesus-inspired reading, maybe lives will be changed through the power Jesus has to do amazing work. Even though my friend still hated what had happened, she had a better perspective on the situation. We both trusted that another person's life would be changed.

Prayer: *Dear Lord, help us to help others when they are in need. Amen*

Thought for the day: Jesus makes transformation happen in unexpected ways.

Tara Regina Lyle (Mississippi, US)

God's Shirt

Read Isaiah 49:8–18

I will not forget you. See, I have inscribed you on the palms of my hands.
Isaiah 49:15–16 (NRSV)

I was studying full-time and trying to hold down a part-time job as a minister. My spouse worked full-time. One day, my toddler son sat on my lap at my desk. He was playing with his cup of juice. I was in the middle of a phone call and typing on my computer. Seconds before a church member came through the door, my son spilled his grape juice all over my shirt. What a mess—upset child, phone call, computer, stained shirt, and now someone at my door! I had the presence of mind to stop typing, to say, 'I'll call you back' and to hang up the phone. As for the church member at my door, she laughed when she saw me. She said, 'You should see God's shirt!' and gave me an understanding smile.

Her remark has stuck with me ever since. God takes on so much—all at once—for our sakes. He listens to our prayers, dries our tears, accepts our complaints, forgives our sins and calms our fears. Getting close to us and our spills is certainly going to mess up 'God's shirt'. We may have our hands full, every hour of every day, but we are continually blessed, knowing that through it all, we are fully in God's hands and always loved.

Prayer: *Thank you, God, for loving us through the messy, difficult, painful times of our lives. We need you, and you never fail us. Amen*

Thought for the day: In times of trouble, I will give thanks that God is always near.

Rob Fennell (Nova Scotia, Canada)

Serving with Faith

Read 2 Timothy 1:3–18

I am reminded of your sincere faith, a faith that lived first in your grand-mother Lois and your mother Eunice and now, I am sure, lives in you.
2 Timothy 1:5 (NRSV)

As a teenager, I was part of a large youth group. The group was made up of young people from ten churches within a radius of 37 miles. Years later, we all still serve the Lord with our respective abilities. We keep working to learn and serve with faith. Some people have remained in their original areas; others were sent abroad by their churches.

We are not young any more. Most of us are married and have children. Some members of our group already have grandchildren. Recently, after 26 years, we held a reunion. We invited our children to participate so that they would know what we had done. We wanted them to be inspired to follow our example of faith and service. At the reunion, we emphasised service and the passionate faith passed from Lois to Eunice and Eunice to Timothy. Likewise, we want to give the spirit of service and faith to our children.

Prayer: *Our Father in heaven, thank you for giving us a chance to do your work. Strengthen us to keep serving you. In Jesus' name we pray. Amen*

Thought for the day: I can be an example of God's spirit of service for others.

M. Iskandar Zulkarnain (Semarang, Indonesia)

God's Constant Presence

Read Psalm 139:7–12

Do not be afraid, for I am with you.
Isaiah 43:5 (NIV)

In 2003, my husband and I decided to move out of our large house where we had lived for 44 years. The house that had been ideal when our three children were at home presented major problems after our retirement. We were full of questions. Where would we go? What would we have to leave behind? How would we pare down all our accumulated possessions?

We found no easy answers. We visited several retirement villages in our city, but none was right for us. In time, however, we found one in eastern Tennessee. The prospects looked good. But we still faced the wrenching challenge of changing our church, friends and activities, as well as the huge task of disposing of our possessions.

With the help of our daughters, we found answers. The baby grand piano would fit into our new tiny living room. Our children could use many of our things. We could have a sale to deal with the rest.

Yet I wavered and wept. Change has never been easy for me. But when our daughter Betsy said, 'Don't worry about moving, Mother, God is already there,' I was able to go forward and not look back. Her words come to me again whenever change challenges me.

Prayer: *Gracious God, remind us that you are always present to help us through times of change and stress. Amen*

Thought for the day: Wherever we go, God is already there.

Carolyn Hodge Rogers (Tennessee, US)

Fake Fishing

Read Matthew 4:18–22
[Jesus said] 'Follow me, and I will make you fish for people.'
Matthew 4:19 (NRSV)

For my tenth birthday I begged for and received a shiny new fishing rod. On my first trip to the brook, I was squeamish about pushing the worm on to the hook, so I quietly decided to use the meat from my sandwich instead. My brother wondered why the fish were biting for him but not for me. I just held my pole up, shrugged my shoulders and smiled. As my brother reeled in his fish and began to clean them, I had a horrible realisation. If I caught a fish I would have to do the same. I quietly pulled in my line, removed the meat and threw the line back in with no bait. I had decided I didn't like fishing. It was more enjoyable to pretend to fish!

I have learned that in my Christian life I sometimes pretend in much the same way. I go through the motions but have no substance. I act as if I am involved but really only give half my heart. I know that if we are to follow Jesus' teachings and offer the Good News to others, we cannot pretend—going through the motions while failing to give our full commitment. Jesus doesn't want pretend Christians. He calls us to pick up our nets and truly follow him.

Prayer: *Gracious Lord, help us to be true to you as you call us into ministry with others. Help us to follow you with courage and conviction. Amen*

Thought for the day: I do not want to pretend to follow Jesus.

Avis Hoyt-O'Connor (Maryland, US)

Burying Your Talents?

Read Matthew 25:14–30

'I was afraid, and I went and hid your talent in the ground. Here you have what is yours.'

Matthew 25:25 (NRSV)

Our interim minister recently preached a sermon on the parable of the talents (see Matthew 25:14–30) that helped me to realise its fuller meaning. Because I had always looked at this parable only in terms of money, I could not understand why the master was so angry at the servant who hid his talent. After all, this servant did not lose the money. But this sermon reminded me that 'talents' can be our God-given gifts, not just money.

My new understanding of the parable made me think of Jesus' disciple Andrew. He was an average, everyday fisherman. But he used what he had to bring new people to Jesus. He brought his brother, Simon [Peter] to meet Jesus (see John 1:41) and found the young man with the five loaves and two fish the day Jesus fed the five thousand (see John 6:8–9).

Thinking about the scripture in this way, it became apparent to me that we can use our God-given gifts for furthering his kingdom, no matter how small they may seem. God can magnify any small talent into something wonderful.

Prayer: *Dear God, thank you for the gifts and talents you have given us. May we put them to good use to your glory. Amen*

Thought for the day: Where can I use my talents for God?

James C. Seymour, Jr (New York, US)

Connected

Read 1 Corinthians 12:12, 21–26

In Christ we, though many, form one body, and each member belongs to all the others.
Romans 12:5 (NIV)

My son is a United Methodist missionary. I have been fortunate to meet many faithful Christians while travelling with or visiting him in other countries. As a result, I feel just as connected to believers overseas as to those in the next town.

I feel close to these Christians because I have faces, voices and smiles to help me connect. Andriy, Nastiya, Sergei and Pavel are real people to me. When I read a meditation in *The Upper Room* written by Pavel, I can remember him and rejoice that he is my brother in Christ. When I pray for these friends, I'm praying for people who I know personally. I have heard their stories.

Not all of us have the opportunity to travel to other lands, but each of us can find brothers and sisters whom God is calling us to love. A local mission trip, a soup kitchen, a ministry to the sick or elderly and other creative ministries all help us to make a connection in the body of Christ with those who were once strangers.

Prayer: *Dear God, help us always to remember our connection to the entire body of Christ. Amen*

Thought for the day: In Christ, we have brothers and sisters all over the world.

Debbie Airgood (Pennsylvania, US)

God is Near

Read Psalm 42:1–5
Why, my soul, are you downcast? Why so disturbed within me? Put your hope in God, for I will yet praise him, my Saviour and my God.
Psalm 42:5 (NIV)

One of the first things I learned as a Sunday school teacher is that one child will always cry for their parents. Sunday after Sunday at least one child dissolves into tears after the people who make them feel secure have left the room.

I gently explain to each child that their parents are nearby, that they were brought to the class to help them learn. It does not mean they have been abandoned or will be separated for very long.

Then, when a particular challenge disrupted my world and left me feeling helpless, I understood how the children felt. As I look back I wonder: why did I fear? Why was life so difficult? Why did I feel lonely? My Lord was nearby, watching over me, but also allowing me to learn and build character.

Now when adversity threatens to make me feel distant from God, I reflect on those distraught children during Sunday school.

With renewed confidence I repeat: 'God is nearby.'

Prayer: *Holy and loving God, strengthen us through your powerful presence in our times of need. Amen*

Thought for the day: I will seek God's presence in all that I do.

Esther Ruiz Saldana (Coahuila, Mexico)

Trusting God

Read Isaiah 40:26–31

Trust in the Lord with all your heart and lean not on your own understanding; in all your ways submit to him, and he will make your paths straight.

Proverbs 3:5–6 (NIV)

Recently, my wife began chemotherapy treatment for the second time in four years. I tried to be content with our situation and rely on God for strength. My daily supplication to God became, 'Please heal her quickly, Lord.' I expected immediate results.

I am grateful that the Lord has blessed my wife and me with many years together, and I hope to be with the Lord someday. But I am still anxious and still rely upon my own understanding as I hope for her quick return to health. Today's quoted scripture verse tells me to look to God for understanding instead. I am trying to trust him with my wife's healing and find joy in the promises and encouragement of scripture. God promises that we can be content even when facing mortality if we rely on Christ for strength.

Prayer: *Dear heavenly Father, give us the courage to face the unknown through our faith in you as we pray, 'Our Father which art in heaven, Hallowed be thy name. Thy kingdom come. Thy will be done in earth, as it is in heaven. Give us this day our daily bread. And forgive us our debts, as we forgive our debtors. And lead us not into temptation, but deliver us from evil: For thine is the kingdom, and the power, and the glory, for ever.'* Amen*

Thought for the day: I can find strength by trusting God.

Gary Kiddie (California, US)

* Matthew 6:9–13 (KJV)

Lost and Found

Read Ephesians 2:1–10

If a shepherd has a hundred sheep, and one of them has gone astray, does he not leave the ninety-nine on the mountains and go in search of the one that went astray?
Matthew 18:12 (NRSV)

I have a special place in my heart for those who have been convicted of breaking the law. I must have 'inherited' it from my father. He worked with people who had been either on probation or incarcerated. He was strict with them, yet caring. He talked with them and tried to help them to change, to get 'clean' and begin to live purposeful and productive lives. My dad told me that most of the people he worked with came from dysfunctional families. All of them, especially teenagers, desperately want to be loved.

Maybe, in addition to my dad's influence, I inherited this empathy from my heavenly Father. While we may see criminals as unworthy, God cares for them; after all, they too are created in his image and likeness. In spite of their wrongdoing, God loves them and seeks them out.

Heaven rejoices when the lost are found. My family knows it first-hand; my brother was one of them. Even though we are all capable of sin, Jesus redeems us by his shed blood—a sacrifice that brings us God's forgiveness. All of us who have lived outside God's law can now live righteously and with purpose.

Prayer: *Compassionate God, we thank you for your loving heart. We want to love you in return by living in accordance with your will. In Jesus' name. Amen*

Thought for the day: 'I once was lost but now am found' (from 'Amazing Grace' by John Newton, 1779).

Yulia Bagwell (Pennsylvania, US)

Spiritual Guides

Read Matthew 7:13–14
You guide me with your counsel, and afterwards you will take me into glory.
Psalm 73:24 (NIV)

My wife arranged a concert at our home to raise funds for a charity working to eliminate human trafficking. Since we live at the end of a cul-de-sac, we were concerned about parking for the visitors. Fortunately, we have a large car park next door, but the only access is through a narrow gap between two knee-high wooden poles. Our solution was for my son and me to stand on either side to guide the drivers in and out.

This made me think about the narrow path that leads to eternal life (see Matthew 7:13–14). Then, I thanked God for the many people who have acted as spiritual guides to keep me on the path of faith. I also thought about how important it is for me to act as a guide for those whose lives I touch. I pray constantly that I will stay on that path that leads to eternal life and that I may lead others to God as well.

Prayer: *Thank you, God, for our spiritual guides. Please help us to act as faithful mentors to others. Amen*

Thought for the day: For whom can I act as a spiritual guide today?

Bill Gosling (Western Australia, Australia)

With God's Help

Read Romans 4:16–21

'I know that you can do all things; no purpose of yours can be thwarted.'
Job 42:2 (NIV)

When Moses told the Hebrew leaders all that God had promised to accomplish, 'They believed. And when they heard that the Lord was concerned… they bowed down and worshipped' (Exodus 4:31). How excited the Israelites must have been, knowing that God would deliver them! Perhaps they imagined a quick, easy exodus. Instead, their predicament got worse. Pharaoh wasn't about to release them simply because Moses told him to; in fact, he imposed tougher demands on them. So rather than bowing down and worshipping God, they complained.

Sometimes I'm like the Israelites. I trust God's leading and joyfully worship. Then the path gets rocky and, instead of turning to God, I complain. Instead of seeing the obstacles as opportunities to trust him, I get discouraged.

Many times in the Bible, circumstances got worse before God's promises became reality: Joseph was imprisoned before becoming a leader; Abraham was asked to sacrifice his son before becoming the father of nations; Paul was blinded before becoming an apostle to the Gentiles. But God continued to work in the lives of these people and continues to work in ours. Knowing that God is always present, we can rejoice and worship even in hard times.

Prayer: *Dear Lord, thank you for your faithfulness. When we struggle, help us to see that you are still at work in our lives. In Jesus' name, we pray. Amen*

Thought for the day: With God's help, I can overcome obstacles.

Georgia Bruton (North Carolina, US)

Active Listening

Read Psalm 119:97–105

[Jesus said] 'My sheep listen to my voice; I know them, and they follow me. I give them eternal life, and they shall never perish; no one will snatch them out of my hand.'
John 10:27–28 (NIV)

I serve as an instructor pilot in the United States Navy Reserve and teach students to fly complex jet aircraft that travel at high speeds. One of the areas in which student pilots encounter difficulty is in learning to listen effectively and understand critical radio communications. Air traffic controllers speak quickly and often use abbreviated terminology, which sometimes makes their communications difficult to grasp. When my students become confused by a radio call they do not understand, I draw on past experience and training to help them translate the controller's instructions. We need those instructions as pilots in order to continue flying safely and to complete our mission.

The challenges faced by my students are not unlike those that we face as Christians trying to carry out God's will. We might be eager and determined to follow God's plan in our lives, but too often we neglect to work on our listening skills. Fortunately, like my students, we have the ability to become better listeners. Training our ears through regular study of the Bible and faithful participation in worship makes it easier to understand the communications God is sending us.

Prayer: *Dear Lord, help us prayerfully and continually to seek your guidance. Help us also to follow that guidance so that we may better serve you. Amen*

Thought for the day: How will I listen to God and others today?

William P. Moynahan (Virginia, US)

A Little Deeper

Read Matthew 14:23–31

Jesus immediately said to [his disciples]: 'Take courage! It is I. Don't be afraid.'

Matthew 14:27 (NIV)

My two-year-old daughter stood hesitantly on the shore, the sea inches away from her feet. 'I'm scared,' she said adamantly. 'It's OK,' her aunt coaxed, 'take just one step.' She took one baby step. 'OK,' said her aunt, 'now just a little deeper.' She took another step and another while trustingly holding her aunt's hand. 'A little deeper, now a little deeper.' In a few moments my daughter was standing triumphantly waist deep in the shallow water. 'I'm in! I'm in!' she shouted excitedly.

I envied her, thinking of all the times I've cheated myself of that same feeling of victory because I'm too scared to follow Jesus out a little deeper. How often have I chosen to stay up on the shore of insecurity? Our insecurities may make so much sense to us, but they keep us on the shore by constantly reminding us of the negative judgements of others. But Christ passes no such judgements. He does not want us to stay on the shore but coaxes us out to where true intimacy and victory can be found. 'Just a little deeper,' he says. I want to feel the same joy my two-year-old felt as she jubilantly played in the waves—the feeling of victory over my fears and doubts and insecurities. But the path to that kind of joy lies out a little deeper.

Prayer: *Dear Lord, grant us the courage to follow you out into a deeper Christian experience today. Amen*

Thought for the day: With Christ's help, we can overcome our fears and insecurity.

Sarah Reeves (Georgia, US)

Awake

Read Proverbs 3:1–6

Indeed, he who watches over Israel will neither slumber nor sleep. The Lord watches over you—the Lord is your shade at your right hand.
Psalm 121:4–5 (NIV)

Our plane was gliding over patches of clouds. After a little while, the crew announced that because of the weather, the flight might be bumpy, but there was no reason to panic. However, I had never been so scared during a flight. I leaned back and closed my eyes.

Suddenly, today's verse echoed in my ears, and I felt something different. Ah! It is God's presence! It was so different, so comforting and reassuring.

I started thinking about the pilot who was awake while some of the passengers were sleeping. He was alert and controlling the aircraft. Our heavenly Father, the Creator and Pilot of the whole universe, never sleeps or slumbers (see Psalm 121:4). We can lean on God without fear. If we surrender ourselves to God's hands, he will faithfully lead us even when we are not sure of the path ahead. I am thankful for God's word and for his eyes upon each of us until the end of our life journeys.

Prayer: *Heavenly Father, help us to lean on you and to trust in your promise. Amen*

Thought for the day: Even when the path seems unclear, God faithfully leads us forward.

Surama Mohapatra (Odisha, India)

Good Times and Bad Times

Read Lamentations 3:19–24

I have learned the secret of being content in any and every situation, whether well fed or hungry, whether living in plenty or in want.
Philippians 4:12 (NIV)

I am going through a prolonged period of unemployment. In the past, I have always been able to find work. But during this current period without work, I have come to accept that I will experience hardships in my life.

Hardships are not necessarily times of judgement or punishment. Good times and bad times are both integral parts of life. I would be naive not to expect hardships; but as a Christian, I can also hold on to hope and trust in God the Father.

Both Job and Paul expressed wisdom in facing hardships. 'Shall we accept good from God, and not trouble?' Job asks (Job 2:10). The wisdom of his statement is subtle and difficult to grasp. Paul writes in Philippians 4:11: 'I have learned to be content whatever the circumstances.' To me, it is a peaceful acceptance that I will experience both hardship and good times. But my trust, faith, and hope are in God, whose steadfast love and mercies are 'new every morning' (Lamentations 3:23).

Prayer: *Dear God, take away our fear as we face hardships. Give us peace in knowing and trusting you. Amen*

Thought for the day: I will look for God's love and mercy today.

William Peoples (California, US)

Join the Dots

Read 1 Corinthians 2:12–13

Faith comes from hearing the message, and the message is heard through the word about Christ.
Romans 10:17 (NIV)

After our morning service, I was chatting to a friend I had encouraged to come to church. He admitted that although he had been attending for some time, he was still not feeling much benefit in his spiritual life, as I had predicted he would.

Why I said it I still don't know, but out of the blue I explained that I had recently bought my grandson a book of dot-to-dot pictures to complete and colour. He'd looked at it and then handed it back. 'I don't understand,' he said. 'There are no pictures.' I showed him that if he joined dot one to dot two and so on, he would uncover a complete picture. Eventually he was excited to discover a picture of a rabbit, which he then coloured in.

I apologised to my new Christian friend for using such a childish example, but suggested that the same could be true for him. Each week he could learn from the things he read and heard at church, asking where he did not understand, until a picture of God began to emerge for him. 'I don't know where you got that from,' he said, laughing, 'but it sums up exactly how I feel. Now I'm going to start at dot one and go on from there.'

I was glad to have helped my friend, but I was amazed and thankful for the way that the Spirit had helped me to find the right words to say to him at the right time.

Prayer: *Heavenly Father, encourage us to read and study your word, and to share what we have learnt with others through your Spirit. Amen*

Thought for the day: How can I share God's word with someone today?

Brian Gaunt (Yorkshire, England)

Calm

Read Matthew 8:23–27

[Jesus] said to them, 'Why are you afraid, you people of weak faith?' Then he got up and gave orders to the winds and the lake, and there was a great calm.
Matthew 8:26 (CEB)

When I had finished my exercise routine, I decided to walk along the beach. At one point I stopped to watch and appreciate the power of a rolling wave as it approached me. I worried I would be soaked by the wave, so I had two options: stay and see what happens or move back. I decided to stay. Slowly the great wave came toward me and then it receded.

We can feel a similar sense of anxiety when circumstances threaten to overwhelm us. We may feel trapped in an emotional and spiritual whirlwind.

When we allow our anxieties to overcome us, we are like the disciples who were frightened during the storm in today's reading. They were witnesses to God's power, and Jesus was among them. Still, their faith failed them. If we learn to depend fully on God's power, we can remain at peace, knowing that all will be well. Even when we see great waves coming toward us, we can trust that little by little they will recede.

Prayer: *Dear God, help us to rely fully on you when we are overwhelmed by the circumstances of our lives. Amen*

Thought for the day: I can have peace and joy when I trust in God.

Eymi Jairon Vásquez Suárez (Dominican Republic)

Listen to Me

Read Luke 10:38–42

Guard your steps when you go to the house of God. Go near to listen rather than to offer the sacrifice of fools.
Ecclesiastes 5:1 (NIV)

As a child, I took lessons in martial arts. Each class began with bowing to the instructor and to the most senior member of the class, out of respect and gratitude for what they would teach us that day. Then we participated in meditation. We were to set aside the day's struggles, emptying ourselves so that we could focus on the commands and instructions of the teacher.

When we read God's word, this same practice of meditation can help us set aside distractions before we begin. We can set aside thoughts of the colleague who annoys us, the broken relationships, the fears about finances. Then we can focus on what God has to teach us. God may indeed teach us about the colleague or our finances, but if we bring all those specific struggles to our reading, we may miss his lesson. That's why Ecclesiastes 5:1 says, 'Guard your steps when you go to the house of God. Go near to listen rather than to offer the sacrifice of fools.' The psalmist proclaims, 'Your word is a lamp for my feet, a light on my path' (Psalm 119:105). If we bring the distractions of our day to our Bible reading, we may end up walking down the wrong path. When we read humbly, with uncluttered minds, ready to listen, God will light each step of our lives.

Prayer: *Dear Lord, open up our hearts so that we can hear you. Help us to be still and quiet so that we can listen to your teaching. Amen*

Thought for the day: When I read the Bible, I will ask God to still all other voices.

Kyle Taft (Tennessee, US)

The Gift of Love

Read 1 Corinthians 13:4–13

Love is patient; love is kind.
1 Corinthians 13:4 (NRSV)

One of my favourite scripture passages is 1 Corinthians 13, and I wanted to read it at my son's wedding. Uncomfortable with public speaking but wanting to give this reading as a gift to the newly-weds, I began preparing by reading it aloud every morning to my husband. And every morning, he joined me in saying the last few words: 'and the greatest of these is love' (v. 13).

As the wedding day drew closer, my husband's health began to deteriorate quickly. It soon became clear that he would not be able to attend the wedding. He needed assistance with bathing, eating and dressing. Putting on a shirt often left him out of breath. He was grateful for the help I gave him, and he expressed his appreciation often. We found ourselves quoting to each other words from the scripture: 'Love is patient; love is kind.'

Ten days after the wedding, my husband passed away. My new daughter-in-law read 1 Corinthians 13 at his funeral. I learned in those days that love is a true gift from above.

Prayer: *Dear God, thank you for your presence in happy times and in trying times. Your love is always patient and kind. Amen*

Thought for the day: God's love for me is always patient.

Elizabeth K. Bush (Maine, US)

Prepared for Action

Read 2 Timothy 2:15–21

Prepare your minds for action; discipline yourselves; set all your hope on the grace that Jesus Christ will bring you when he is revealed.
1 Peter 1:13 (NRSV)

Sunshine and warm temperatures were expected on Monday, and I had planned to do some gardening. But when Monday arrived, I could find only one gardening glove and my small spade was nowhere to be seen. Frustrated by my unsuccessful search for what I needed, I gave up on the task I had planned to complete.

Just as it is important to be prepared for physical tasks like gardening, it is also important that I am prepared mentally and spiritually each day for the tasks God has in store. I can't always know ahead of time what 'God-appointments' I will have on a given day, but I can prepare my mind for action. Through scripture, prayer and the expectation that God will throw unforeseen tasks my way, I can be prepared ahead of time. And when I'm ready, I'm more apt to obey.

Recently I felt the nudge to telephone the mother of my son's friend to invite her son to a church event. I made the call because my mind was prepared for action. The young man came with us and had so much fun that he hopes to return.

God honours our preparation by allowing us to be the sowers of seeds for his reign on earth.

Prayer: *Dear God, help us to prepare our spirits so we are ready when you place a task before us. Amen*

Thought for the day: I will prepare myself to answer God's call.

Kim Harms (Iowa, US)

The Spirit Intercedes

Read Romans 8:18–27

The Spirit helps us in our weakness. We do not know what we ought to pray for, but the Spirit himself intercedes for us through wordless groans.
Romans 8:26 (NIV)

For years, I had trouble praying. The problem was not in the actual act of prayer but in the fear that I wasn't praying correctly. I had received so much advice on different ways to pray that I was afraid of not making myself understood. In the midst of a minor crisis in which I wanted to communicate that I needed God with me no matter what happened, the Spirit led me to dwell on Romans 8:26. I finally understood. The words I use are not all that important; I simply need to pray. God knows what is happening in our lives and what we need. And the Holy Spirit helps us to pray, giving voice to all we are trying to say.

Since then, praying has been easier for me. Sometimes I pray in new or different ways. Even when I feel muddled, I now understand that the Spirit intercedes, making my prayers clear to God.

Prayer: *Thank you, Father, for an intercessor who assures us that when we pray you know what we want to say. As Jesus taught us, we pray, 'Our Father which art in heaven, Hallowed be thy name. Thy kingdom come. Thy will be done, as in heaven, so in earth. Give us day by day our daily bread. And forgive us our sins; for we also forgive every one that is indebted to us. And lead us not into temptation; but deliver us from evil.'* Amen*

Thought for the day: I can rest in the promise that the Spirit intercedes for me.

Donald Lett (Ohio, US)

* Luke 11:2–4 (KJV)

Power of a Psalm

Read Psalm 121

I lift up my eyes to the hills—from where will my help come? My help comes from the Lord.
Psalm 121:1–2 (NRSV)

During our son's training as a cadet in the US Air Force, he and the other cadets were tested to their limits. As his parents, we supported him during those trying days. We wrote to him, prayed daily for him, and encouraged him to draw strength from Psalm 121—a favourite scripture passage of ours. That psalm spoke directly to him there in the Colorado mountains when the psalmist said: 'I lift up my eyes to the hills—from where will my help come? My help comes from the Lord.' We often encouraged our son to look up to the mountains that surrounded him and to remember this psalm.

Upon completion of his basic training, he said that our encouragement and the spiritual strength he drew from this passage—and his own personal faith—had enabled him each day to face tough challenges with renewed confidence. Throughout his years as a cadet, our son continued to draw inspiration from the Lord through regular worship in the air-force chapel. All during his 20 years as a pilot, he knew that God was near.

When we face difficulties, such as disease, loss of a loved one, or the loss of a job, we can turn to Psalm 121 and lift our eyes to the Lord with the assurance that God will help us and sustain us.

Prayer: *Thank you, O Lord, that we can always look to you, knowing that you are with us and care about us. Amen*

Thought for the day: Wherever I am, I can seek God's help.

Donald Huffman (North Carolina, US)

The Joy of Obedience

Read Deuteronomy 28:1–6

All these blessings will come on you and accompany you if you obey the Lord your God.

Deuteronomy 28:2 (NIV)

Recently, I saw a student tilting his chair back in class. I reminded him that another student had fallen while doing the same thing and had needed to go to hospital for stitches. I told the student not to tilt the chair, and I continued helping another student with his mathematics. A few minutes later, when the student who was tilting back his chair fell off it, I was reminded of how often characters in the Bible struggled to obey God.

In scripture, God calls us to obey because obedience will lead to blessings. Moses challenged Israel in today's reading to 'carefully follow all [the Lord's] commands' (v. 1). Moses reminded Israel that in keeping them, 'all these blessings will come on you and accompany you' (v. 2): their cities would be blessed; their families and farms would be blessed. They would experience abundance. Moses concluded, 'You will be blessed when you come in and blessed when you go out' (v. 6).

A life of obedience to God requires much and is difficult at times, but the path leads to joy and blessings.

Prayer: *Father God, help us to obey your commands, especially when we find it difficult. Thank you for our joys and blessings. Amen*

Thought for the day: How can I be obedient to God today?

Mary Ng Shwu Ling (Singapore)

Never Forgotten

Read Joshua 1:7–9

[Jesus said] 'Look, I myself will be with you every day until the end of this present age.'
Matthew 28:20 (CEB)

While walking along the lakeside of our local county park, taking photos of the beautiful landscape, and enjoying the sunshine and warm breezes, I noticed something lying on the grass. It was a child's tiny toy truck—rusty, dented, apparently abandoned and forgotten by its young owner. As someone struggling with depression, I often feel the same way: cast aside and forgotten. But God's word reminds me that's not so!

When Moses died, leaving Joshua with the overwhelming responsibility of leading the Israelites into the promised land, God encouraged Joshua by promising: 'As I was with Moses, so I will be with you; I will not fail you or forsake you' (Joshua 1:5).

And in John 14, Jesus prepared his disciples for his imminent departure. 'Do not let your hearts be troubled,' he told them (v. 1); and a little later on, he promised, 'I will not leave you orphaned; I am coming to you' (v. 18).

At times, we may feel as though no one cares about us, making us think we have been abandoned and forgotten. But we can take comfort in the truth of God's promise never to leave us or forsake us.

Prayer: *Dear God, thank you for your loving, faithful presence in our lives, even when we can't feel you here with us. Amen*

Thought for the day: Because God made me, he never forgets me.

Pamela Manners (New Jersey, US)

Pestering God

Read Luke 18:1–7

You who call on the Lord, give yourselves no rest and give him no rest.
Isaiah 62:6–7 (NIV)

'Oh please, Mummy! Please! Oh please!' I said. When I was a child and wanted my mother to say yes, I pestered her constantly. She often told me to stop, that she had heard me already and was considering my request. But it was hard for me to be quiet; pleading for something I wanted seemed to be in my nature.

Some years ago, one of my own children was struggling, and I was concerned. I prayed about it constantly. I couldn't let it go. My concern was so great that I found myself thinking I must be driving God crazy, the way I used to drive my mum crazy when I pestered her.

Then to my amazement and relief, I discovered Jesus' parable in Luke 18:1–7. God is not bothered by our constant prayers. How reassuring to know that he wants us to bring our concerns over and over again! Today the situation I was so concerned about has been resolved. But of course, I'm still pestering God. Now I smile and thank the Lord for letting me voice my concerns in prayer over and over again.

Prayer: *Heavenly Father, thank you for your patience. Ease our burdens as we bring them to you in prayer. In Jesus' name we pray. Amen*

Thought for the day: God always welcomes my prayers.

Harriet Michael (Kentucky, US)

Unmistaken Identity

Read Isaiah 43:1–7

[The Lord says] 'Do not fear, for I have redeemed you; I have called you by name, you are mine.'
Isaiah 43:1 (NRSV)

One Sunday the assistant at a local shop smiled at me broadly as she added up my bill. As she handed me my change, she said, 'Have a great day, John!' I was puzzled at how she knew my name. Then I realised that I was still wearing my name tag from church.

Our name tags list the name of our church and today's quoted verse from Isaiah. By wearing these name tags, church members hope to help newcomers to learn people's names and feel welcome. The quote on the tags also reminds the wearer and the reader that God has called us each by name. I realised that by wearing my name tag, I was sharing this message of welcome with people in the shop—and I didn't even realise it!

After this experience, I now make a point of wearing my church name tag in public places before and after our worship services. My name tag makes me more aware that people may notice my behaviour, and so I am mindful that I may be the best example of a Christian that someone might see that day. This practice reminds me that God has called each of us by name to be living examples of his love in Christ, no matter where we are.

Prayer: *Dear Lord, you have called us by name to be your people. Help us to proclaim your gift of salvation in Christ to the world. Amen*

Thought for the day: How do I show others that God has called me by name?

John Blossom (Connecticut, US)

Wings of Time

Read Ecclesiastes 3:1–8

Forgetting what is behind and straining towards what is ahead, I press on towards the goal to win the prize for which God has called me heavenwards in Christ Jesus.
Philippians 3:13–14 (NIV)

Butterflies of excitement fluttered within me as I sat to open the large pile of birthday cards. Everything about this birthday seemed big. I'd never before received so many cards or such a large array of presents, or been given such a huge arrangement of flowers. But one thing loomed extra large—my age!

One by one each card reminded me of time gone by. The number of years ahead of me were far fewer than those now behind me. The years seemed to have grown wings! A touch of apprehension began to mingle with my excitement as I contemplated the future.

Then I smiled. A friend's handwritten note urged me to think not of lost youth but of the new opportunities ahead. I recalled Paul's words in Philippians: 'Forgetting what is behind… I press on towards the goal.' I felt my apprehension melt away, leaving only the butterflies of excitement.

Each decade of life heralds a new season in life. Whatever our age we can step forward with confidence as we journey hand in hand with the Lord towards our ultimate destination.

Prayer: *Lord, help us not to cling to the past but to keep hold of your hand and trust you for each day. Amen*

Thought for the day: Life with Jesus is always an adventure.

Julia Cutting (Yorkshire, England)

Giving from the Heart

Read Luke 21:1–4

'Truly I tell you,' [Jesus] said, 'this poor widow has put in more than all the others.'
Luke 21:3 (NIV)

Forty years ago, when I lived in the United States, I learned about an organisation that helped poor children all over the world. But as a single mother of three, I myself was too poor to make a contribution. Then in 1976, God called me back to Iceland to teach the Bible here. We were still poor, but in 1978 God made it possible for me to be a sponsor for children around the world. The first child I sponsored was a girl in India. Since then I have sponsored children in Mexico, Honduras, Guatemala, Rwanda, Barbados, Thailand, as well as on Native American reservations.

At the age of 77, I still sponsor four children. I am encouraged by today's reading in which Jesus teaches us that it's not the size of the gift that matters to God but the generosity of the giver's heart. My small contribution sustains two children in Uganda for a whole month! I contribute what I can, and I thank God for the joy I receive from helping these children.

Prayer: *Dear Lord, do not let us forget the hungry people in this world, but help us to remember that even small contributions can make a big difference. Amen*

Thought for the day: God makes all things possible.

Sonja R. Haralds (Iceland)

If Only They Knew

Read Romans 2:1–6

His delight shall be in the fear of the Lord. He shall not judge by what his eyes see, or decide by what his ears hear.
Isaiah 11:3 (NRSV)

I was driving with my foot to the floor. The speed limit was 50 mph, but my car would not go any faster than 20 mph. Several drivers glared as they sped past me. Some had clenched fists, uttering words I thankfully couldn't understand. They had no idea that I was going as fast as my car would allow. I was unfairly judged solely by what they saw.

Circumstances and situations aren't always as they appear. When relevant information is missing or overlooked we all make assumptions. I learned what it's like to be on the receiving end of unmerited judgement. God used this incident to humble me and to reveal the sin in my own heart. It was time for me to repent and turn away from my sin.

How often do we jump to the wrong conclusions because we failed to get all the facts? How often have our thoughts about others been judgemental? Instead of judging others, we can delight in God's goodness and begin to learn how to extend his grace to others in their times of need.

Prayer: *Dear Lord, let our hearts search beyond what our eyes see so that we are careful not to pass judgement on others. Amen*

Thought for the day: I will not make unfair judgements today.

Lydia Gomez Reyes (Texas, US)

From Death to Life

Read John 5:24–26

[Jesus said] 'Anyone who hears my word and believes him who sent me… does not come under judgement, but has passed from death to life.'
John 5:24 (NRSV)

I was helping to take care of my sister, Josephine, who had a terminal condition. For two weeks my duties had included showing her love by listening to her, helping her to eat and assuring her that God was present with her. During one of the visits, the nurses asked me to stay by her bedside even after visiting hours. I was grateful for the extra time with my sister.

While I was there, my sister asked me to help her to have a bath. As I helped her dress, took her back to bed and tucked her in after the bath, I remember thinking that she was getting well. Josephine then whispered, 'Violet, you can go now. God will bless you.' As I was on my way home, I was called back to the hospital. On arrival, I was ushered into a waiting room and told that my sister had died shortly after I had left. Though I felt great pain, her last words consoled me, 'God will bless you.'

I never imagined that I would have the privilege of hearing someone's last words, and these words reminded me of what I had been taught in Sunday school about Jesus' seven last sayings. The seventh one, 'Father, into your hands I commit my spirit', means that Jesus knew where his spirit would be going. Like Jesus and my sister, anyone who knows and obeys God can face death with the assurance that they will soon be resting in his arms.

Prayer: *Dear God, thank you for your promise that in Christ Jesus we have eternal life with you. Amen*

Thought for the day: In the face of death, God offers eternal life.

Violet Mutasa (Harare, Zimbabwe)

God in the Words

If you ask someone who writes and does it well, they will tell you it's the hardest work a person will ever do. I am inclined to agree. I have dug a ditch on more than one occasion. Digging a ditch is hard work; writing is harder work.

Sometimes—more often than I would like to admit—I wonder why I keep at it. I have a drawer full of manuscripts that no one is likely ever to set eyes on—my rejects, as it were, that would probably be best used to start a fire. I sit before a blank sheet of paper feeling tired before the task has even begun, and I think to myself, 'OK, this is it. I've had enough. This time I am done.' But somehow I always manage to keep going. I always do it one more time.

Occasionally I write something decent, something I think may be worth a second glance or another pair of eyes. At other times I read what I have written and throw it away. But whatever the result, good or bad and for better or worse, I keep writing.

I suspect I keep writing because my closest encounter with God occurs through words on a page. It is in language—whether my own or others'—that I am most aware of God's presence and most confident that he is there.

In short stories, poems and novels, I meet God in the words, sentences and paragraphs that express the complexity, strangeness and beauty of human life. I encounter God in the mystery and depth of a good story and in the intelligence and creativity of a clever poem. I encounter him in the rhymes of an old hymn, in a well-written sermon, and, of course, in scripture itself.

My relationship with God begins in language. I was not there to witness the events I read about in scripture and which give meaning to all that I do. I can only enter those events through language—the exceptional prose of the book of Ruth, the speeches of Job and his friends, the proclamations and oracles of the prophets, Jesus' parables and Paul's letters. All words.

More times than I would like to admit, I have doubted God's presence in my own circumstances or the circumstances of others. 'Where are you, God?' I ask. 'You may be somewhere, but I don't see you here.'

In these moments of doubt, I turn to scripture. I turn to the narratives and metaphors and characters that have endured for thousands of years. And I am reminded that God was there when the words were written and that he is still in them now.

I am reminded of God's presence in the pages of this magazine too, in all the stories of pain and joy, doubt and hope, self-revelation and universal application that you share. Language links us together. And I suppose that, when it comes down to it, this is what keeps me writing—the hope that one day someone else might read what I have written and, in a time of confusion or doubt, confidence or certainty, find God's presence there.

When I read the devotional submissions that come across my desk, I remember that God is still with us because he is everywhere in the words of *The Upper Room* writers and in the words we pray with millions of people around the world. If I accomplish nothing else, I would hope that my words written here will also help to bring you, our readers, closer to God.

Several meditations in this issue address God's presence in our lives and our awareness of that presence. You may want to read the meditations for 5, 17, 25 and 30 September; 4, 8, 12, 15 and 25 October; 9 and 21 November, and 18 and 31 December before responding to the reflection questions below.

Questions for Reflection:

1. Recall a time when you doubted God's presence. What was occurring in your life at the time? Who or what helped you to reconnect with him?

2. Can you think of a time when you were very aware of God's presence? What was that experience like for you?

Andrew Garland Breeden
Associate/Acquisitions Editor

Peace in Suffering

Read Romans 5:1–5
Since we have been justified through faith, we have peace with God through our Lord Jesus Christ.
Romans 5:1 (NIV)

In his last days, my father-in-law suffered from severe bronchial problems and most of the time had to be connected to a breathing apparatus. His distress became ours as family members stayed by his side and cared for him constantly.

Despite his acute health crisis he showed spiritual maturity and reliance on the Lord, especially by reminding us constantly of the verse quoted above. My father-in-law had given his life to serving the Lord, both in the mission field and pastoral ministry. It was a blessing for all the family members to observe the way he remained faithful and never lamented his suffering. Instead, he encouraged us to remain at peace, to continue to place our trust in God's work.

As we devote our lives to service and remain faithful through our times of suffering, then we, too, can gain the peace that only God can give.

Prayer: *God of eternal life, give us the peace that only you can provide through our faith in Christ. Amen*

Thought for the day: The peace of God surpasses all understanding (see Philippians 4:7).

Raul Rocha (Buenos Aires, Argentina)

Open to God's Guidance

Read Exodus 3:7–10

The Lord said, 'I have observed the misery of my people… I have come down to deliver them.'

Exodus 3:7–8 (NRSV)

We were on our way from Tennessee to Alabama. The beautiful stretch of road promised smooth driving, until a huge sign indicated a detour. We took a left turn and ended up on a very different road. We waited at crossroads and stopped at stop signs. The satnav invited us to turn right and then to turn left. As we drove through neighbourhoods, we were confused. However, remembering the guidance given by the sign on the main road, we advanced until we were directed back to it.

Our detour made me think of Moses. His routine was changed when God told him to go to Pharaoh and to bring the Israelites out of Egypt. I thought of the many instances when, along the journey to the promised land, the confused and fearful people criticised Moses' determination to get them to their destination. With every hardship, the people complained, leaving Moses to struggle, wondering what his next move would be. But God offered new possibilities and reminded Moses of his mission.

Some of life's experiences sidetrack us. Others bring us to a crossroads. They bring us to places of doubt and questioning. God extends an invitation to be open to his guidance, especially in times of doubt and confusion.

Prayer: *Gracious God, in the midst of doubt, give us grace to trust your guidance. Amen*

Thought for the day: Today I will listen for what God is inviting me to do.

Stephane Brooks (Tennessee, US)

Seasons of Life

Read Isaiah 41:5–10
[God] has made everything beautiful in its time.
Ecclesiastes 3:11 (NIV)

Last week I had dinner with an old friend. During our conversation, my friend said she realised that we are in the autumn of our lives. Initially this made me feel sad, as I sometimes fear the passing of time and the thought of death. The reality is that most of my life is behind me now.

But this morning, I am sitting here looking out of my window at the glorious display of golden leaves falling from the large maple tree in our front garden. The sun highlights the leaves as they gently fall, and I am reminded that autumn is my favourite season. It's a time for slowing down and gathering in. I am spellbound by the beauty of God's plan for the cycle of nature and the seasons of life. So I will try to be at peace in this autumn of my life. It is a beautiful season, with a colourful mix of joy and sadness.

God still has work for us to do, so we can slow down, sit quietly and listen for guidance. We can trust in God's perfect timing and assurance to be with us in our fears. We can find comfort in his promise of eternal life through Jesus Christ.

Prayer: *Gracious God, we thank you for the beauty of your earth and for the seasons of our lives. Help us to come to you with our fears, knowing that you will strengthen and uphold us. In Jesus' name we pray. Amen*

Thought for the day: God is with us during all the seasons of our lives.

Betsy Thompson (Indiana, US)

Spider Town

Read Leviticus 26:1–13

Your heavenly Father knows that you need all these things. But strive first for the kingdom of God and his righteousness, and all these things will be given to you as well.

Matthew 6:32–33 (NRSV)

After the rain, the sun shone low across the path as I walked toward my home on a late summer's morning. This path is bordered by tall close-clipped evergreen hedges, all festooned that morning with row upon row of finger-length webs—small glistening hammocks, each one hiding its builder, a tiny spider.

I thought briefly of this community of spiders, who were concerned only for their essentials, revealing another example of God's amazing creation.

And then I thought of the many different human communities in our world, each with individual stories to tell. I thought of the residents of the homes around me, and those in the apartments nearer the city centre. I thought of the early morning busyness and the anticipation of a new day; of the worries of illness and people looking for work; of the stress of strained relationships; of children who are neglected.

As I walked and prayed for all of these people, I thought of my own life and my communities and gave thanks to God for my health and well-being. I thought of ways I might be able to meet the needs of those around me, and I praised God, our Creator and Saviour.

Prayer: *Dear Lord, help us to see the needs of those around us and to respond as you would. Amen*

Thought for the day: Today I will look for new ways to serve my community.

Brian Beeson (Derbyshire, England)

Never Give Up!

Read James 1:2–6

We know that suffering produces perseverance; perseverance, character; and character, hope.
Romans 5:3–4 (NIV)

During my teaching career I decided to pursue National Board Certification, a rigorous and demanding endorsement. Teachers are allowed only three attempts to pass the certification process. My two young children and my husband supported me emotionally and encouraged me.

Year-one results came in; I did not make it. I was saddened and weary, knowing I had to endure the process again and wait an entire year for the new results. Year-two results came in; I did not make it. Finally, in the third and last year I achieved my goal.

I knew through those three difficult years my children were watching my actions and how I handled failure. I wanted them to know that God gives us the strength to persevere, that when you fall you get back up and keep trying.

That three-year trial taught me a lot about endurance and made me a better person. I thank God for this experience and the opportunity to bear witness to my children that from our trials come strength of character and hope for the future.

Prayer: *Thank you, God, for giving us opportunities in our struggles to gain character and hope. Help us to never give up, even when we feel defeated. In Jesus' name we pray. Amen*

Thought for the day: Whether I win or lose, my perseverance will produce a godly character.

JoAnn Tumbleston Jarman (South Carolina, US)

In the Belly

Read Jonah 1:1—2:10

[Jonah prayed] 'I went down to the land whose bars closed upon me for ever; yet you brought up my life from the Pit, O Lord my God.'
Jonah 2:6 (NRSV)

God told Jonah to deliver a warning to the Ninevites. But the Ninevites were Jonah's enemies, and the last thing he wanted was to preach God's message to them. So Jonah ran and hid from God. Not until after he had been cast off a boat and swallowed by a big fish did Jonah begin to pray. But rather than giving up on Jonah, God had already provided that fish to save him. What Jonah considered punishment, God had sent as a miracle to save his life.

Jonah's story became my story when I began to run from God. Eventually, I made the biggest mistake of my life: stealing money from an employer who trusted me. Like Jonah, I was running away from my faith and trying to solve my problems alone—without God. And just as with Jonah, God sent me a lifeline; but in my case the 'belly' where I found myself was prison. Though initially I saw it as punishment, this event was a miracle from God. While I have been in prison, he has put me back on the right path. Now I have a stronger and richer relationship with him than I ever had before.

God never gives up on working through us. He is not finished with me, and I thank him daily for bringing me back to my faith. None of us can run or hide from a God who is all-knowing and who never gives up on us.

Prayer: *Dear God, thank you for the miracles you bestow on us and for never giving up on us. Amen*

Thought for the day: When I'm in the 'belly' of a troubled life, I can call on God who perseveres in loving me.

Daniel Klahn (California, US)

I Am Who I Am

Read Exodus 3:10–15

God said to Moses, 'I AM WHO I AM.' He said further, 'Thus you shall say to the Israelites, "I AM has sent me to you."'

Exodus 3:14 (NRSV)

A dear family member recently suffered an illness that left her practically incapacitated. Friends and family members flooded her with questions about the hows and whats of her condition. After wrestling with how to relate the complex medical information, she finally resolved to say, 'It is what it is.'

In the midst of life's challenges, we sometimes wrestle with the hows and whats of a solution. We can be confident of God, that he is who he is. God is the 'I am', who is present when we need him to be with us in our current circumstances.

Whether we need a counsellor, a comforter, a guide or provider, God addresses us: 'I am who I am' (Exodus 3:14). Even though we may not be aware that God was present at the time, we can rest assured that he is actively working in our situation.

Prayer: *Dear God, we praise you for being ever-present, trusting you to be with us in all circumstances. We pray as Jesus taught us, saying, 'Our Father in heaven, hallowed be your name, your kingdom come, your will be done, on earth as it is in heaven. Give us today our daily bread. And forgive us our debts, as we also have forgiven our debtors. And lead us not into temptation, but deliver us from the evil one.'* Amen*

Thought for the day: I will trust God to be with me in my circumstances.

Christy Bailey (Illinois, US)

Behind the Scenes

Read John 2:1–11

[Jesus'] mother said to the servants, 'Do whatever he tells you.'
John 2:5 (NIV)

I love weddings. I am sometimes asked to arrange the flowers or make bouquets for the event, so I am often one of the many busy people behind the scenes. People work hard to prepare for weddings, so I often wonder what went wrong at the wedding in today's reading that they ran out of wine. Had someone miscalculated how much would be needed? Had more guests than expected attended? Had the wedding feast lasted longer than planned? We don't know the reasons; but whatever they were, Jesus' mother trusted him to solve the problem. It is good that her instructions to the servants were so insistent, because his request was very strange. Imagine their surprise when what came from the jars had mysteriously become wine.

Jesus solved the problem that no one else at the wedding could. When we encounter difficult problems in our lives or the lives of others, we would love a solution. As Christians, we know asking Jesus for help is the best way to solve our problems. Like Jesus' mother, we can trust that Jesus will guide us to do what is right, even if it seems strange or illogical. Jesus' solutions will be better than ours.

Prayer: *Dear Lord, give me a heart to serve others, eyes to see when you are performing miracles and a desire to behave as kindly as you do. Amen*

Thought for the day: When I serve others, I can witness God's miracles.

Fiona Massie (Oxfordshire, England)

24/7

Read Romans 8:31–39

Neither death nor life, neither angels nor demons, neither the present nor the future, nor any powers, neither height nor depth, nor anything else in all creation, will be able to separate us from the love of God that is in Christ Jesus our Lord.

Romans 8:38–39 (NIV)

A friend asked me, 'What have you learned about God that you didn't expect to learn?' After taking some time for reflection, I replied that when I first accepted Christ I viewed God as someone who was always there but only to be called upon when absolutely needed. My thinking was that I shouldn't overuse the privilege of talking with God or overload him with specific prayers. Maybe I thought that my requests shouldn't compete with all the other prayers that were surely more significant than mine. I thought my interaction with God should follow the instructions on the sign I have seen in public places: 'Use Only in Case of Emergency'.

Over the years, as I've tried to grow in my Christian faith, my perspective has changed dramatically. I now believe that God wants to be part of my life at all times, 24 hours a day, 7 days a week. We were created to know him. I still struggle with comprehending that the God who created the universe also wants to be in constant fellowship with me. But I know it's true; that's how much God loves us. We can do our part in the relationship through prayer, meditating on the word and striving to live a life that's pleasing to God.

Prayer: *Loving God, we rejoice that you created us to know you. Help us to seek a deeper relationship with you each moment of every day. Amen*

Thought for the day: God is with us and wants a relationship with us 24/7.

John D. Bown (Minnesota, US)

Held up to the Light

Read Ephesians 5:6–14

So if anyone is in Christ, there is a new creation: everything old has passed away; see, everything has become new!
2 Corinthians 5:17 (NRSV)

Recently I came across a pile of vintage tablecloths that I had collected over the past several years. A cherry-print tablecloth caught my eye. As I unfolded it and ran my hands across the fabric, I felt a rough patch. I walked over to the window, holding it up to the light.

Oh! Look at those small holes! What had been hidden when the cloth was folded among the others was totally exposed when held up to the light. When I examined each cloth individually, I found tiny holes, water stains and fabric frays.

Like the tablecloths, I look pretty good when I am in a crowd. I blend in, and my imperfections are hidden fairly well. My sharp tongue and critical spirit don't stand out. When I compare myself to others, I seem OK. But on my own, I realise I am far from perfect.

I am comforted by the promise in the verse quoted above. The light of Christ makes all things new. What a good and gracious God we have who recreates our lives!

I continued to examine the tablecloths, no longer disappointed. Some could still be used; the stains on others would wash away. Others would be cut and reshaped for another use. In the same way, Jesus offers us new life and a new purpose.

Prayer: *Light of the world, reveal our sins and make us into your new creations. Amen*

Thought for the day: No matter what my sins are, God can restore me.

Connie Gochenaur (Indiana, US)

Never Thirst Again

Read John 4:10–14

'Whoever believes in me, as Scripture has said, rivers of living water will flow from within them.'
John 7:38 (NIV)

On a day trip, we stopped in a small village. Our children asked why we were there. 'Let's go and get a drink,' we said. They thought we would buy soft drinks at the local shop, but we surprised them.

Just past the shop, there was a fountain coming out of the ground. Water bubbled out of it in a steady stream. Each child drank from the fountain while the others giggled and expressed surprise. 'Where does it come from?' they asked.

We explained that an underground spring had been tapped and a pipe constructed so that everyone could enjoy the supply of fresh, cold water.

Jesus promised that those who believed in him would possess streams of living water. The promise meant that in the future, believers would be filled with the Holy Spirit. We drink living water from Christ; and we are filled and satisfied, overflowing with the Spirit of eternal life.

Though this spring may one day dry up, the Holy Spirit is an everlasting source of refreshment. Because of our faith in Jesus, living water is a promise we can always be sure of.

Prayer: *Dear God, help us to be a source of refreshment to those who are in need of your love. Amen*

Thought for the day: God is a constant source of refreshment.

Paula Geister (Michigan, US)

God Provides

Read Romans 12:1–8
The word of the Lord came to Elijah: 'Leave here, turn eastward and hide… You will drink from the brook, and I have directed the ravens to supply you with food there.'
1 Kings 17:2–4 (NIV)

When I was in college I had very little money. One Sunday morning I used some of what I had to get to church. While I was in church I felt called to give an offering, and I decided to give all that I had left to the church. I did not think about how I would get back from church or how I would eat that day. I gave what I had to God and continued to worship. After the service, someone approached me and gave me enough money to cover the costs of my day, and even more.

This event inspired me to think about the way God provides for us. In today's scripture, the prophet Elijah fled without taking anything to eat or drink because God promised to send ravens to bring him food. God can help us in unexpected ways and can use anyone or anything around us as instruments of care for us. When we give our best, God will give us more than we can imagine.

Prayer: *Dear Lord, teach us to understand and believe in your promise to provide for us, so that we will not hesitate to give our best to you. Amen*

Thought for the day: God can send other people to help me.

Peter Hulu (Yogyakarta, Indonesia)

The Stoning of Stephen

Read Acts 7:55–60

[Stephen] kneeled down, and cried with a loud voice, 'Lord, lay not this sin to their charge.' And when he had said this, he fell asleep.
Acts 7:60 (KJV)

When I read the story of how Stephen was cast out of the city and stoned to death because of false testimony brought against him, I often wonder how he could still pray for his killers. Instead of praying that the Lord would stop the stoning, Stephen asked that their sin not be held against them. I also pause to think: what would have happened if Stephen had not prayed for his killers?

When Stephen prayed to God for mercy for his killers, he prayed for their souls. I believe this compassion for his killers must have been sent from God. When I see and hear of all the evil in the world, I wonder: do I pray only for the victims or should I pray for the people responsible for the evil?

Stephen's story reminds us to pray not only for strength and hope for the victims but also for mercy for those responsible for the evil. God sent Jesus to redeem the soul of everyone, so we can pray for each person as a precious creation of God.

Prayer: *Dear God, fill me with compassion to pray for those who would do me harm. Amen*

Thought for the day: Today I can pray for someone who has hurt me.

Margaret McMillin (Texas, US)

Planting the Seed

Read 1 Corinthians 3:6–11

I planted, Apollos watered, but God gave the growth.
1 Corinthians 3:6 (NRSV)

Since I have a great love and zeal to minister to young gang members, I decided to visit an area of town where I encountered one of the most notorious gangs. In my mission to reach everyone, I requested the use of the community centre in our neighbourhood so I could invite them to enjoy some snacks and soft drinks. Even though these young people knew I would be sharing God's word with them (something I assumed would be boring to them), they still felt a sense of importance at being the only invitees, with the refreshments an added bonus. Eventually, through God's grace, I succeeded in starting a dialogue with a few gang members who were willing to hear God's word.

Over time in these gatherings, the Bible became a seed—planted and nurtured by the prayers of many who desired to see change in the lives of these young people. Without a doubt it is God who gives the growth and helps us to guide others along the right path.

Prayer: *Lord of all, may the word we speak in your name give new life to those who hear it. Amen*

Thought for the day: What can I do today to bring God's word to others?

Patricia Rivas (Valle del Cauca, Colombia)

Expectant Prayer

Read Ephesians 3:20–21

In the morning, Lord, you hear my voice; in the morning I lay my requests before you and wait expectantly.

Psalm 5:3 (NIV)

A friend was telling me about a Christian concert at which she was going to sing. She and others had spent long hours organising and practising for the event. Worry began to show on her face as she confided in me that she had hoped for 200 people to attend but expected only about 50. I told her to continue to pray and then to expect amazing results. The night of the concert came, and people began to enter the church—217 of them!

Beautiful music filled the air, and the message of God's love was felt by everyone who listened.

This experience caused me to wonder how often I pray without expecting an answer. When I pray I always hope for the best, but in reality I haven't always expected the best. I've come to understand that God's answer may not be revealed immediately or may be different from what I was hoping for. But I can trust that God's answer will always be the best answer for me.

Prayer: *Dear Father God, thank you for hearing us and for helping us to wait in expectation. Amen*

Thought for the day: God never leaves prayers unanswered.

Jerry Bragalone (Pennsylvania, US)

When There Are No Words

Read Job 2:11–13

The prudent keep their knowledge to themselves, but a fool's heart blurts out folly.
Proverbs 12:23 (NIV)

'I can't imagine how you must feel.' The grief my friend experienced when her husband died was palpable, but I realised there was nothing I could say to make it better. Sometimes the insecurity we feel for not saying the 'right' thing can lead us to say the 'wrong' thing.

Jewish tradition has held that mourners are to keep silent until the bereaved person speaks. It's a good practice because it can give us time to consider what we should say, preventing us from saying something that is not helpful. Even after this time of silence, our responsibility to choose our words with care remains. Job's friends may have been silent until he spoke; but when they did speak, their questions turned into accusations against Job and God. Their words were tinged with judgement and blame, causing Job even more pain.

Like Job's friends, I have often felt the need to offer my opinion or question circumstances in an attempt to explain God. Such an attitude has done little to show me and others who God is. By listening to God's guidance we can discern when and how to comfort those who are hurting.

Prayer: *Teach us, Lord, to sit quietly with those who are grieving. Fill us with peace so that we can comfort them in their time of sorrow. Amen*

Thought for the day: Sometimes God's greatest comfort comes through our silent presence.

Deanna Baird (Michigan, US)

Advertising in Public

Read Mark 5:1–20

[Jesus] said to them, 'Go into all the world and preach the gospel to all creation.'
Mark 16:15 (NIV)

I was travelling by bus when a well-dressed young man stood up and started talking about a new herbal product. He was moving from the front of the bus to the back, making sure all could hear him. I appreciated this man's courage. He had a job to do, and he did it with conviction. He did not worry what passengers thought of him or whether his continual babbling disturbed them. In the end two people bought the product. He waited a few more minutes before getting off the bus, probably to board another and continue selling his product.

In today's reading the healed man wanted to accompany Jesus, who had given him a new life. But Jesus asked him to go back and share the goodness of God with his family and friends. So he went proclaiming his healing in the Decapolis and people were amazed. He obeyed the Lord.

The same command to share the good news is given to all who have received new life in Christ. We may not all go to far-off places or public gatherings to proclaim the gospel, but we can share it with our family members, friends, colleagues and others we meet in everyday life.

Prayer: *Dear God, give us the courage to share the good news with others. Thank you for helping us overcome shyness, hesitation and fear so that we can share the message of your love. Amen*

Thought for the day: Today I will not hesitate to share the good news.

Pramila Barkataki (Assam, India)

Traffic

Read Luke 12:22–31

Seek his kingdom, and these things will be given to you as well.
Luke 12:31 (NIV)

It was a beautiful autumn day. My wife and I were travelling through the hills of North Carolina on our motorcycle. I was anxious about our trip. We needed to reach our destination by the end of the day, and we had decided to take the scenic route to stay off the faster, busy motorway.

As we rounded a bend, we saw two lorries on the road ahead of us. As we approached them I had to pay much more attention to traffic. I began to think I wouldn't get a chance to enjoy the scenery on this trip. I was relieved to find that the trucks moved along swiftly, because the chance of passing one, let alone both, on the winding road of the Appalachians seemed slim.

Suddenly, their progress slowed. A third, heavily-loaded lorry had pulled in ahead of them. My wife and I began to accept that it would be a slow trip. But around the next corner, a long stretch of road without oncoming traffic gave us ample time to pass all three slow-moving vehicles.

I began to think about how often I become anxious when I want God to grant my prayers to suit my own agenda. The clear, straight road ahead reminded me that when we trust God, we can let go of the anxiety and enjoy the journey.

Prayer: *Father, thank you for listening to our prayers. Help us to listen for your answer and direction. Amen*

Thought for the day: I can rely on the Lord's direction.

Raymond W. Appel (Wisconsin, US)

Doing Good

Read Romans 7:7–25

I do not do the good I want to do, but the evil I do not want to do—this I keep on doing.
Romans 7:19 (NIV)

When my daughter was two or three years old, she threw the normal tantrums of a child. When she got into trouble, she would start crying and loudly repeating, 'I want to be good.' I was intrigued by her response.

Paul wrote to the Romans about the same problem. He wanted to do good. He knew what was expected of him and worked to be an example to other people. It was not easy. He was human and imperfect.

We are also meant to be examples. We know what is expected of us; but because of sin, doing good is not easy. God knows we are weak and gives us grace so that we are forgiven when we fall short. When we read the Bible for guidance and pray for forgiveness, he will bless us.

Prayer: *Dear Lord, we want to do good, but sometimes temptation overcomes us. Please guide us and give us the strength to follow you. Amen*

Thought for the day: With God's help, I can 'be good'.

Marqueta Reedy-Engle (Ohio, US)

God's Markers

Read 2 Thessalonians 3:1–5

May the Lord direct your hearts to the love of God and to the steadfastness of Christ.

2 Thessalonians 3:5 (NRSV)

In 1920, the United States opened its first coast-to-coast airmail delivery route. Before radio navigation was common in aeroplanes, pilots had to navigate by landmarks. Therefore, bad weather and night time essentially grounded them. The solution was to build a system of concrete arrows—stretching 70 feet along the ground—every ten miles from New York to San Francisco. Each arrow had at its centre a steel tower with a beacon on top. As long as the pilots followed the markers they would reach their destination. But if they veered off, they might have difficulty finding the route again.

Similarly, God has given us a system of markers to direct our way, including the commandments, promises, precepts and teachings in God's word. They are the stories of the Bible's people and the gift of Jesus Christ. They guide us through life; when we wander away from them, we become lost and confused. They lead us straight to God's love and forgiveness.

As solid as aviation's 70-foot concrete markers were, most of them are now gone. In contrast, God's truths will endure eternally. We can entrust our lives to such markers, knowing they will lead us directly to the heart of God.

Prayer: *O God, help us listen for your voice in scripture—the voice that calls us and leads us through our lives. Amen*

Thought for the day: Where is God guiding me today?

Bob La Forge (New Jersey, US)

Helping Hand

Read Psalm 139:1–10

If I could fly on the wings of dawn… [to] the far side of the ocean—even there your hand would guide me; even there your strong hand would hold me tight!
Psalm 139:9–10 (CEB)

My great-grandniece started walking at the age of ten months. To develop this new skill and feel more secure, she would hold on to someone's hand. Because she was persistent, the process of learning to walk went faster than it might have done.

Learning to walk the Christian path is much slower than learning to walk physically. The good news is we don't have to travel it alone. When we take the hand of God, we can feel secure. The challenges we face become more bearable when we lean on our sisters and brothers in the faith.

In today's reading, the psalmist expressed confidence that God knows us completely—knows our innermost thoughts and the words we have yet to speak. But most important to me is knowing that God is with us and that his hand rests upon us. It is something so sublime that we cannot fully understand it. But we can rest assured that wherever we go, God's strong hand will guide us.

Prayer: *Thank you, God, for your promise to help us and to guide us. Amen*

Thought for the day: God can use my helping hand to guide others today.

Luciria Aguirre Naranjo (Valle del Cauca, Colombia)

Letting Go

Read Isaiah 43:16–21

One thing I do: forgetting what is behind and straining toward what is ahead, I press on toward the goal to win the prize for which God has called me heavenward in Christ Jesus.
Philippians 3:13–14 (NIV)

As I pulled up my once-beautiful periwinkles, now lifeless after a recent freeze, it dawned on me that I wasn't just getting rid of the old plants, I was making room for new ones. The same is true of life's experiences. We have to let go of the past to make room for the future. But letting go of treasured moments or painful experiences is not as easy as discarding wilted, lifeless periwinkles.

The apostle Peter wanted to remain in a powerful moment while high atop the mount of transfiguration (see Matthew 17:1–4). Peter was like many of us; he didn't want to let go of an awesome experience. Such moments—life's great blessings—are not meant to be permanent homes but rather rest stops along life's journey.

Painful moments are even more likely to bar us from future joys. But how do we move on? We do it by focusing on God, whose grace and blessings are new every day. And we can find and enjoy them fully when we let go of the past and trust the God of our present and our future.

Prayer: *Dear God, give us the grace to let go of the past and the faith we need to look forward to the future with you. Amen*

Thought for the day: Letting go of the past enables me to embrace God's possibilities.

Eddie D. Fleming (Kentucky, US)

Hungry and Thirsty

Read John 7:37–39

[God] has filled the hungry with good things but has sent the rich away empty.
Luke 1:53 (NIV)

'Come on, boys; dinner's ready!' My daughter called her two young sons to the table. James came running and sat down, looking to see what delicious food his mother had prepared. Jonny came slowly, bringing some of his toy cars to the table. 'Put them away now, and eat up,' said Mum. Jonny wriggled on his seat but made no effort to do what she said. 'Jonny's been eating sweets from his friend. He doesn't want any dinner,' said James smugly. 'He ate the whole bagful.' Jonny had come to a feast already full of food.

Sometimes, like Jonny, I need more discipline in my life. It is so easy to fill my life with books, television and other kinds of entertainment so that I don't have much of an appetite for God. Most of these pastimes are not bad in themselves, but they satisfy me only for a short time. I want to come hungry and thirsty to the feast of love God continually spreads for all.

Prayer: *Dear Lord, we come to your table hungry and thirsty for you. Thank you for giving us nothing less than your own self. As Jesus taught us, we pray, 'Father, hallowed be your name, your kingdom come. Give us each day our daily bread. Forgive us our sins, for we also forgive everyone who sins against us. And lead us not into temptation.'* Amen*

Thought for the day: What is pulling my attention away from God?

Marion Turnbull (Liverpool, England)

* Luke 11:2–4 (NIV)

Thanksgiving Every Day

Read Philippians 4:4–7

Rejoice in the Lord always. I will say it again: rejoice!
Philippians 4:4 (NIV)

In my country we celebrate a day of thanksgiving each year. I wonder how many people stop to consider why they celebrate. Does a day of thanksgiving cause us to pause and evaluate what we are truly thankful for?

As Christians, should we—could we—have thanksgiving every day? In 1 Thessalonians 5:18, Paul writes, 'In everything give thanks.' The apostle is not saying that we are to give thanks *for* everything, but *in* everything—despite the circumstances. We know it is not easy to thank God in the midst of trouble, but we are not alone. God is there with us in the midst of our struggles, guiding us through.

An attitude of praise and thanksgiving is a choice, an act of our will. Sometimes we will not feel like giving thanks. But consider the results of doing so: a change takes place in us and around us; things begin looking up. We can cultivate an attitude of thankfulness and have thanksgiving every day.

Prayer: *O God, we pray that your love will grow in us each day. Help us learn to give thanks in all situations. Amen*

Thought for the day: What can I thank God for today?

April James (California, US)

Freedom to Choose

Read Romans 11:25–36

According to God's choice, they are loved for the sake of their ancestors.
Romans 11:28 (CEB)

Every day we are required to make choices: when to get up, what to eat, how to approach the day. Many of our choices are major decisions about the road we will travel in life. Our environment, education, goals, friends and heroes all influence our choices.

As a parent, I made many decisions for my child in his early years; gradually, as he grew older, I allowed my son to begin making his own choices. No matter what I thought, he had to start deciding what road he would walk.

The disciples made a choice. Jesus called to Simon and Andrew, 'Come, follow me,' he said, 'and I'll show you how to fish for people' (Mark 1:17). Jesus offered them a choice that would direct the rest of their lives.

God gives us free will to choose our direction in life. We can choose to pray daily, to read the Bible, to attend church or to extend kindness to a stranger. When we learn to put our faith in God and to allow him to guide our lives, we can have confidence in the choices we make.

Prayer: *Thank you, God, for the wisdom you give us each day. May we use it to make good choices and to give you the glory. Amen*

Thought for the day: Today I will seek God's wisdom for every choice I make.

Clay Vincent (Montana, US)

PRAYER FOCUS: SOMEONE WHO HELPS ME MAKE GOOD CHOICES

Trusting God

Read Proverbs 3:1–8

Trust in the Lord with all your heart and lean not on your own understanding; in all your ways submit to him and he will make your paths straight.
Proverbs 3:5–6 (NIV)

My father was a minister in another part of the country and truly devoted to the church. He had diabetes and was dependent on insulin. One day, after visiting him, I prayed that God would not let my father die alone. Three weeks later, on a Sunday morning, I received a call that he had been found dead in the church office. I felt hurt and angry that he had died alone, and that no one had checked on him. I was also angry with God because I felt that he had not heard my prayer. I wept.

Then I remembered the verse quoted above. Although I was still angry, I sought comfort through prayer and reading the Bible. I cried out to God as I read my Bible, many times falling asleep with it in my arms. Soon after my father's funeral, I began to feel God's peace again.

Trusting God is about having faith that no matter what happens his word is true—and then obeying that word. God welcomes us when we're hurt, lonely, afraid or just don't know what to do. Whatever we experience—whether the loss of a loved one or problems in our jobs, in our homes or in relationships—we can trust in God.

Prayer: *Dear God, help us to believe in you and to obey your word regardless of how things appear, trusting in your love and faithfulness. Amen*

Thought for the day: When everything looks bleak to me, God's understanding surpasses mine.

Yolando S. Cooksey (California, US)

First Sunday of Advent

Read Luke 5:12–15

It came to pass, when he was in a certain city, behold a man full of leprosy: who seeing Jesus fell on his face, and besought him, saying, 'Lord, if thou wilt, thou canst make me clean.'
Luke 5:12 (KJV)

In today's reading, we find a man confronted with bad news: he has been struck by a painful and incurable disease. Leprosy is a disease whose effects are visible on the skin: blemishes, wounds and bruises that in severe cases disfigure the body. Can we find any good news in such a painful situation? Yes! Jesus' power shines in the midst of the greatest darkness.

The presence of Jesus was the first good news to the man with leprosy. Simply because the Lord was there, the man rediscovered hope—something lost long ago. 'Lord, if thou wilt, thou canst make me clean' was his cry. Lying prostrate on the ground meant grief, deep sadness. And that man had reason to feel that way. But at the same time, he believed that Jesus could heal him.

This remains good news for us today. In the presence of the Lord we can always hope. However great our pain and problems or the difficulties and darkness in our past, Jesus has the power to restore.

Prayer: *Dear God, thank you for your healing power in our lives. Grant us the strength to come to you in the face of good news and bad. Amen*

Thought for the day: I can find hope for healing in Jesus.

Antonio Wilson (Inhambane, Mozambique)

'Please, Lord, Fill Me'

Read Isaiah 35:3–10

Jesus said to [the crowd], 'I am the bread of life. Whoever comes to me will never be hungry, and whoever believes in me will never be thirsty.'
John 6:35 (NRSV)

As a former water-utilities instructor travelling throughout West Texas, I've seen drought many times—up close and personal. To me, drought is scarier than almost any other natural disaster. When fires or floods hit, we can survey the damage and then start cleaning it up. But drought is like a cancer, slowly and steadily depleting the land. Day after day, the sun bakes the land; the crops and fields wither and die, and eventually even the very earth dries up and blows away. I remember the people of one small town with a tiny lake as their only source of water. As the water level crept lower and lower, somebody had affixed a homemade sign to the depth gauge with a message that said it all: 'Please, Lord, fill me.'

It takes a very determined faith to last through such times. But it is worth it when the rains finally do come. Literally overnight, the skies clear and the dust settles. Then, land that just a few days before had been a desert begins to bloom again. It's always true. We may dig holes in the ground of faith, but only God can fill them with the water of life.

Prayer: *Dear Lord, help us to remember always that no matter how barren our lives may seem, you can always make them green again. Amen*

Thought for the day: In times of spiritual drought, God can fill me with hope.

Mark A. Carter (Texas, US)

Showing Love

Read Matthew 25:31–46
The King will reply, 'Truly I tell you, whatever you did for one of the least of these brothers and sisters of mine, you did for me.'
Matthew 25:40 (NIV)

As I was walking home, I saw three young girls who looked confused. They asked me, 'Sister, do you want to cross the road?' I replied, 'Oh no, I'm waiting for the bus.' They looked sad and disappointed. Then I asked them, 'Children, where do you want to go?' They said, 'We want to buy something in the supermarket across the road, but the road is very crowded and we are afraid.'

I am sometimes frightened when crossing the road too. But on that day, I immediately reached for their hands and helped them across. I was afraid amongst the busy traffic, but I knew God would help us. The children thanked me and I felt a strong sense of joy. With God's help I was able to show love to the three girls.

Sometimes we think we cannot do anything to help others. But I believe that with God's strength we can do much more than we can imagine. God is pleased when we offer love and compassion, no matter how insignificant our actions may seem. He calls each of us to show love to the world.

Prayer: *God of mercy, help us always to act with love toward others in need. In Jesus' name. Amen*

Thought for the day: Our acts of compassion shine God's love into the world.

Linawati Santoso (East Java, Indonesia)

Healing Prayer

Read James 5:13–16

Confess your sins to each other and pray for each other so that you may be healed. The prayer of a righteous person is powerful and effective.
James 5:16 (NIV)

Three-and-a-half hours elapsed as my sister's friends and family waited in the crowded hospital waiting room.

We were relieved when the doctor made her way toward us. She explained that the operation had gone well, but she also had bad news. As she was sewing up the incisions, the needle had broken off and disappeared into my sister's stomach. Our hearts plummeted. The doctor assured us that she and her colleagues would find it quickly with the help of X-rays and by possibly widening the incision. After the doctor had left, my cousin suggested that we pray. Soon, others in the waiting area started talking and praying for one another. This moment drew us together as we realised that praying for one another can bring healing to our souls.

About an hour-and-a-half later, the doctor returned. 'I can't explain it, but the needle rose to the surface, and we were able to get it straight away!' she said. Everyone in the waiting room clapped. A lady sitting next to me said, 'Our prayers were answered!'

God answers prayers every day. He wants us to come together in love and concern for one another. When we reach out to one another in unity of spirit, we share the healing love of God and its power to bring us peace.

Prayer: *Dear heavenly Father, thank you for being with us and answering our prayers. Help us to know that your love and grace are more than sufficient. Amen*

Thought for the day: The prayers of others are gifts from God.

Terrye Blevins (Michigan, US)

Desires in Conflict

Read Romans 7:14–25

I do not do the good I want to do, but the evil I do not want to do—this I keep on doing.

Romans 7:19 (NIV)

I was alone in a foreign country, on an overnight stopover after a busy three weeks of preaching and teaching, and I had once again watched TV pornography. No one will know, I'd rationalised; but when I returned home, I felt ashamed and told my wife. I had degraded the holiness of our sexual intimacy, objectified women and disrupted trust in my marriage. My outer life reflected my desire to serve Jesus. But my inner life focused on me and on what I wanted; and I indulged my sinful nature. I experienced an inner conflict. 'The evil I do not want to do—this I keep on doing,' wrote the apostle Paul (Romans 7:19). Paul understood my struggle.

I know that many people wrestle with the temptation of pornography. Dealing with temptation is a constant effort to check our natural desires, to maintain closeness to the Lord and to be trustworthy in our relationships. In my case, I felt so much shame that I joined a Christian group for men with similar struggles. Through accountability and prayer, my outer actions gradually began to conform to my inner hopes and intentions. Slowly, the Lord enabled me to overcome my sinful desires. Like Paul, we all participate in a battle between our fleshly desires and our intentions to be spiritual. God through Jesus Christ rescued Paul. Christ rescued me and will do the same for all of us.

Prayer: *Dear God, lead us to Christian friends with whom we can talk about our most difficult struggles. Amen*

Thought for the day: Christ can work through our fellow Christians to rescue us.

Richard Sims (US)

Doing What is Right

Read Proverbs 21:1–21

Whoever pursues righteousness and kindness will find life and honour.
Proverbs 21:21 (NRSV)

Recently, I was struggling with feelings of uncertainty and a lack of direction; in general I wasn't sure how I felt. My uncertainties were frustrating and affected nearly everything I did. I felt detached from my home life. My work was affected because I felt removed from it as well. Focusing on my work was difficult. I kept asking myself, why? Why am I doing this? Who cares whether I accomplish my goals? I finally took my problem to the Lord. Instead of asking myself questions, I asked God.

As I prayed and listened for God, Proverbs 21:21 came to mind. What a balm to my spirit! God knows my direction and goals and cares about me no matter what. My job, according to the scripture verse, is to pursue righteousness. I can make it my duty to live with love and mercy and to do what is right. Life won't always be easy, but if we work to 'pursue righteousness and kindness', then we 'will find life and honour'.

Prayer: *Dear Lord, sometimes we get confused and we're not sure what to do. Guide our steps toward the path of righteousness so that we can live abundantly. Amen*

Thought for the day: God cares about me no matter what.

Margie J. Harding (Maryland, US)

Worthy is the Lamb

Read John 1:19–31

[Jesus said] 'You shall love the Lord your God with all your heart, and with all your soul, and with all your mind, and with all your strength.'
Mark 12:30 (NRSV)

We all know how hard it is to accept criticism, especially when we're fully convinced that we're in the right. When we get back that best-written essay from our tutor, we cringe at all the critical remarks in red ink in the margin! But, in the course of time, we learn to appreciate criticism given in love: from our spouse or from true friends who are willing to point out the faults in us and call for change.

Such a friend is John the Baptist. As we make ready to receive Christ who comes to us in every moment of our lives, we remember John's call to turn around and make a new beginning in our lives every day. John's is a baptism 'of repentance for the forgiveness of sins' (Luke 3:3, NIV), a repentance that calls us to shift away from our attachment to passing things to focus on what truly matters. John carefully points out to his followers that he is not the one they should look for. He is simply a preacher pointing to the ultimate source of life in all its fullness—Jesus—as he proclaims, 'Here is the Lamb of God who takes away the sin of the world!' (John 1:29).

In this season of Advent we take stock of the things that demand our attention and loyalty and return to our commitment to Christ, the ultimate source of joy and peace.

Prayer: *O God, grant us the wisdom to recognise the lesser things and turn around to adore you as our ultimate source of life. Amen*

Thought for the day: Today, I will turn from what is lesser to what is greatest: Jesus Christ.

M. Thomas Thangaraj (India)

Second Sunday of Advent

Read Matthew 26:26–28

If anyone speaks, they should do so as one who speaks the very words of God. If anyone serves, they should do so with the strength God provides, so that in all things God may be praised through Jesus Christ.
1 Peter 4:11 (NIV)

I volunteer to speak in Sunday services for residents of a nearby care home. Preparing a short sermon can be challenging. The message must be concise and easily understood by the listeners.

One day after my sermon, Holy Communion was offered. An elderly man in a wheelchair declined to take the bread and wine. 'I didn't bring money to pay for it,' he said in a raspy voice.

'That's all right. It's free,' the server said.

What wonderful, glorious news, I thought. We cannot buy the salvation represented by these elements. All we need to do is to believe in Jesus and accept his free gift. This is the heart of the gospel, plain and simple. And it is the best sermon of all.

Opportunities to share this good news of God's word are all around us. We simply have to recognise them and respond.

Prayer: *Dear Father, thank you for the gift of salvation. Help us to hear and receive your good news. Amen*

Thought for the day: How can I freely give what I have freely received from God?

Virginia Horst Loewen (Pennsylvania, US)

Right Hand, Left Hand

Read Colossians 3:23–24
Do not let your left hand know what your right hand is doing.
Matthew 6:3 (NIV)

My wife had surgery on her right hand and couldn't use it for several weeks. She needed help to do almost everything, so I became her right hand. Some of the work and chores were unfamiliar and I did them poorly. This experience helped me understand the idea of the left hand not knowing what the right hand is doing. Nevertheless, my wife encouraged me as I took on difficult tasks, and as the weeks passed, I got better. Now that my wife is well and doesn't require constant help, we are closer for having worked together during that time.

Doing God's work is similar. God chooses to involve us in the divine work. Even after years of trying to do his will, I am sometimes tempted to shy away rather than risk doing a poor job. When this happens, God gently encourages me to pick up the task I am called to. Through the years I have found that the more often I try, the better I get at doing God's work. None of my efforts have been perfect; in fact, some of them have been pretty poor. But God always seems to take pleasure in the results of faithful service.

Today, when God calls me to do something, I enter into the task in prayer and faith. After years of being part of his work, I feel a closeness to my Creator that would not have come any other way. That closeness adds assurance and comfort to each day.

Prayer: *Dear God, thank you for calling us into your service and for accepting our efforts. Teach us to give our best to you and trust you for the results. Amen*

Thought for the day: Everything I do for God matters

Gale Richards (Iowa, US)

Peace That Passes Understanding

Read Psalm 18:31–36

The peace of God, which passeth all understanding, shall keep your hearts and minds through Christ Jesus.
Philippians 4:7 (KJV)

My friend Helen was expressing her concern for her son, who lived in a home for people with disabilities. At 86, she and her husband knew they would not be with David for many more years. I offered what seemed like a helpful response. 'You've done all you can for David. Give your worries to the Lord. Let God take the burden from you.' Helen seemed encouraged, and I was glad to be of comfort to her.

The next day, I received a call telling me that my mammogram showed an abnormality. A repeat test offered confirmation, and a biopsy was ordered for a week later. My words to Helen came back to me. Give your worries to the Lord, I said to myself; but fear flooded my mind, and I couldn't let go. In full panic, I emailed prayer requests to my family and friends. Within hours, I was inundated with assurances of prayer from caring people.

By evening, an amazing peace came over me. I can't control the outcome, I thought. What happens is in God's hands now. If the abnormality is benign, I'll have wasted precious time worrying. If it's malignant, with the Lord's help, I'll get through it. The Bible promises God's peace. Our job is to trust the Lord.

Prayer: *Dear Lord, we find comfort in knowing that when life is difficult, you take away our worries and give us peace. Amen*

Thought for the day: 'Peace I leave with you, my peace I give unto you' (John 14:27).

Betty Rosian (Pennsylvania, US)

Like Trees Walking

Read Mark 8:22–26

Jesus laid his hands on his eyes again; and he looked intently, and his sight was restored, and he saw everything clearly.
Mark 8:25 (NRSV)

Being the youth leader at my church is not easy for me. I have not raised teenagers of my own and do not have any training in working with young people. But this role has given me experiences that have transformed my Christian walk.

One day last autumn, instead of having Sunday school at church, we loaded the teenagers into our cars and visited a nearby nursing home. When we got there some of our group talked, laughed, sang and even danced with the residents. Others went to visit those who were bedridden. I saw one youngster bend over and greet a gentleman with tender words. In another room, another girl sat by the bed of an elderly lady and placed a small cross in her hand. She smiled, and they spoke about her faith in Christ. In the main hall, one teenager played his guitar for the residents.

I realised that I had not seen the potential in these young people; but that day I began to see more clearly, like the blind man in today's reading. Jesus did not give up on that man, and he did not give up on me. In the actions of the young people that Sunday I saw a vivid example of the power of Christ's love to transform each of us.

Prayer: *Dear Jesus, help us to share your love with others. Thank you for all the opportunities you give us to see your love in the world. Amen*

Thought for the day: Today I will look for the potential God sees in others.

Brenda L. Saldana (Puerto Rico)

God's Direction

Read Matthew 7:7–12

A person's steps are directed by the Lord. How then can anyone understand their own way?
Proverbs 20:24 (NIV)

As my college graduation approaches, I have a million thoughts running through my mind: Where will I work? Where will I live? How will I pay my bills? My time at college has taught me that life is uncertain but that God provides.

After my first year of college, I had to take a year off to make money so I could return. I had no work experience, but God provided. I got a good job at a local hospital that paid well and allowed me to work nearly 70 hours a week. It wasn't long before I made enough money to return to college, and my boss let me continue to work during my holidays. That job was God's provision to allow me to finish paying for my education.

Today's verse reminds me that I don't need to have all the answers straight away. I can trust that God will lead me to opportunities. He has always been faithful to me and my family, and we believe in the promise of today's scripture reading that he cares deeply for each of us and our needs. God loves us and will provide a way for us.

Prayer: *Dear God, help us to trust in you and to follow where you lead. Amen*

Thought for the day: How has God led me to where I am today?

Michael Eaton (Texas, US)

PRAYER FOCUS: STUDENTS STRUGGLING TO PAY FOR THEIR EDUCATION

Wind and Waves

Read Mark 4:35–41

Jesus asked them, 'Why are you frightened? Don't you have faith yet?'
Mark 4:40 (CEB)

My two younger brothers, my mum and I went canoeing. When a speedboat went by, the waves rocked our canoe from side to side. I became nervous, fearing that the canoe would tip us into the deep, cold, black water, and we would have to swim a long way back to shore.

In Mark 4:35–41, the disciples were on a boat in rough water. They cried to Jesus, 'Teacher, don't you care that we're drowning?' (v. 38). Jesus replied calmly, 'Why are you frightened? Don't you have faith yet?' (v. 40).

As I remembered the story in Mark 4, I knew that the disciples had experienced a similar thing. They trusted in Jesus, and the storm calmed. When life leads us into rough waters and we are nervous and scared, we can remember to put our faith in Jesus. When we fully trust him, we won't be afraid.

Prayer: *Dear Lord, give us faith in you so that we are not afraid of stormy seas, as we pray, 'Our Father which art in heaven, Hallowed be thy name. Thy kingdom come. Thy will be done in earth, as it is in heaven. Give us this day our daily bread. And forgive us our debts, as we forgive our debtors. And lead us not into temptation, but deliver us from evil: For thine is the kingdom, and the power, and the glory, for ever.'* Amen*

Thought for the day: What fears can I release to God today?

Maya Schroeder (Montana, US)

PRAYER FOCUS: THOSE WHO ARE ANXIOUS OR AFRAID

* Matthew 6:9–13 (KJV)

Steadfast Motivation

Read Hebrews 10:19–25

Let us hold unswervingly to the hope we profess, for he who promised is faithful. And let us consider how we may spur one another on toward love and good deeds.
Hebrews 10:23–24 (NIV)

Anyone who knows my father-in-law, John, knows he loves God. He is also never at a loss for words. Sometimes he makes astute observations. Sometimes he simply reminds people of an important godly truth. At other times he makes humorous remarks, but he always gets people to think. John is a motivator! At his 80th birthday party, I described him as a steadfast stimulator. Hearing John talk spurs others to love and good deeds, as the writer of Hebrews encourages Christians to do.

Jesus also steadfastly provoked deep thought. He moved the woman at the well into assertive action (see John 4:29). He encouraged Nicodemus to ponder how someone can be reborn (see John 3:4). And he motivated a centurion to ask for the healing of his servant (see Matthew 8:8).

Jesus is faithful, and he encourages us to follow him, step by step, with steadfast trust. Whenever we talk to people we encounter, we can encourage acts of love. With Jesus as our model, we can always seek—through our words and deeds—to overcome evil with good (see Romans 12:21).

Prayer: *Dear God, fill our hearts with your faithfulness and love, and help us to motivate and encourage others. In Jesus' name we pray. Amen*

Thought for the day: Today I will celebrate God's promises by encouraging others.

Mark Quick (California, US)

Third Sunday of Advent

Read Luke 2:25–32

[The Lord says] 'You, Bethlehem Ephrathah… out of you will come for me one who will be ruler over Israel, whose origins are from of old, from ancient times.'

Micah 5:2 (NIV)

I often eagerly anticipate birthdays, special outings and holidays. The excitement grows, and then the day arrives. Sometimes I enjoy the event as fully as I expect to, but sometimes the event falls short. Either way, the special occasion passes by and we're left with memories and maybe some photos. The day cannot be relived.

How different is the expectation of the coming of Christ! Through many generations his birth was foretold by prophets, and yet when Jesus was born there were no widespread celebrations. In fact, the inn had no room for him. But some shepherds and wise men, Simeon and the prophet Anna (Luke 2:25–38) quietly celebrated his coming. Later, others recognised Jesus Christ as the long-expected Messiah and went out to preach the good news.

Today we also look forward to Christmas as we celebrate Jesus' birth. But when Christmas Day is over, the reality of the incarnation and the promise of eternal life continues. Each year the Christmas season comes and goes, but what we are really celebrating endures for all eternity!

Prayer: *Father God, thank you for sending your Son to earth to give us the hope of eternal life with you. Amen*

Thought for the day: God exceeds all my expectations.

Elaine Chipps (Western Cape, South Africa)

Diligence

Read Romans 12:6–8

Paul wrote to Timothy, 'Do not neglect the gift that is in you… Put these things into practice, devote yourself to them.'
1 Timothy 4:14–15 (NRSV)

Once more, I removed a sheet of paper from the sketchpad on which I was painting so I could start again. The angel I had been trying to paint looked more like a cartoon character than a celestial being. For many years, I have been painting and then reproducing a watercolour scene for the Christmas cards I send to friends and relatives. 'Why is it so hard this Christmas?' I asked myself. 'Why do I have to begin again so many times?'

As I stared at the blank page in front of me, the answer came to me. It was because I had not painted regularly throughout the year. Without consistent practice, I almost had to relearn my technique. In a sense, I had neglected my gift.

When writing to Timothy, Paul encouraged him not to neglect his gift. Paul knew that when we don't use the gifts God has placed within us, our faith will not grow and strengthen and the ministry God has for each of us will suffer. One of my goals this year is to paint more regularly. But more importantly, I seek to be faithful in using all the gifts God has given me.

Prayer: *Dear Lord, help us to value the gifts you've given us by putting them into practice. Amen*

Thought for the day: Faithfulness requires that I use the gifts God has given me.

Beverly Varnado (Georgia, US)

Choosing the Light

Read 1 John 2:7–17

When Jesus spoke again to the people, he said, 'I am the light of the world. Whoever follows me will never walk in darkness, but will have the light of life.'
John 8:12 (NIV)

Sometimes when our family are travelling we carry camping equipment with us. We try to find somewhere suitable to set up camp while it is still daylight. That makes it far easier to find somewhere pleasant for us to eat a meal and stay for the night.

It is possible to choose a safe site and set up a tent in the dark, but it is far more difficult without the help of daylight. At one site we chose in the dark, we woke the next morning and were alarmed to find dingo tracks in the dry creek-bed beside where we had camped—not a spot we would have chosen in the light!

Sometimes our lives reflect a struggle similar to finding a good campsite in the dark. At times I try to live in my own limited light. It is possible but difficult, and I eventually realise why my life has become such a struggle. I then choose to stop ignoring Jesus' presence, love and strength, and choose to live in Christ's light once again.

Life is so much easier and richer when we live in the light of Christ. We can see where we are going and know that there is someone beside us, guiding and supporting us.

Prayer: *Loving Jesus, thank you for your light which shows us the way. Help us always to strive to live in your light. Amen*

Thought for the day: Jesus is with me to guide and support me.

Meg Mangan (New South Wales, Australia)

Unsentimental Christmas

Read Matthew 2:1–18

Let us throw off everything that hinders and the sin that so easily entangles… fixing our eyes on Jesus, the pioneer and perfecter of faith. For the joy set before him he endured the cross, scorning its shame, and sat down at the right hand of the throne of God.
Hebrews 12:1–2 (NIV)

If I could omit one part of the New Testament, it would be the story in Matthew 2:16–18. I wonder why Matthew included it when Mark, Luke and John were able to tell the good news without including this horrific account. Perhaps Matthew did not want us to confuse sentimentality with hope. Perhaps God inspired Matthew to include this story, knowing that later readers would live in a world where the Holocaust, the killing fields of Cambodia, Rwandan genocide, and unrelenting war in Syria are realities. A birth that did not give hope even in the face of such horrendous events would not be powerful enough to redeem this world.

Matthew gives us the unsentimental version of Christmas. It is not a Christmas that pretends that evil does not exist or that promises a small holiday from evil. The birth of Christ demonstrates to us that while evil is entrenched in the world, it is not in charge. So in the end, however much it disrupts my sentimental view of Christmas, I really am glad this story is in the Bible. It shows me that even at the darkest moment, God gave birth to hope through Jesus Christ.

Prayer: *Come, Lord Jesus, into our hearts and into the world with the hope that only you can offer. Amen*

Thought for the day: Rather than ignoring the sorrows of the world, I can look to Christ for hope.

Michael A. Macdonald (North Carolina, US)

Reaching Out

Read Philippians 4:10–20
My God will meet all your needs according to the riches of his glory in Christ Jesus.
Philippians 4:19 (NIV)

After knee surgery, I had a difficult recovery. I live alone and quickly found that I simply could not manage on my own. I do not like to ask for help and worried that I would be imposing on others.

When I finally reached out for help, I was overwhelmed by the outpouring of support from my church, neighbours and colleagues. All of my worries were calmed. I felt only love.

I have never hesitated to ask God for help, and I know that often he sends people to help us. Scripture assures us that God will always meet our needs, and I have found this to be true. So why was it so hard for me to ask my friends directly when I needed them?

Scripture encourages us to be God's hands and feet on earth in caring for one another. But this experience taught me that a caring relationship is a two-way street. Just as we are often so willing to help, we can also be open to receive from those willing to help us.

I'm fully recovered. But I have learned that when we struggle to make it on our own, God guides the people in our lives to help us. All we have to do is ask.

Prayer: *Thank you, heavenly Father, for always providing for our needs. Help us to realise that we can turn to the people close to us whom you have sent. Amen*

Thought for the day: How can I accept God's help?

Ruby Truax (Ontario, Canada)

Ken

Read Isaiah 30:18–21
It is God who works in you to will and to act in order to fulfil his good purpose.
Philippians 2:13 (NIV)

'I prayed someone would visit me today!' said my housebound friend, Ken. I was nearly in tears; it had only been a thought during the morning service that I should go and see him. I could have ignored it. But sometimes God guides us when we are hardly aware of it.

A week later I sat by Ken's bed in a hospice, almost in silence. As a young Christian I didn't know what to say when he asked me to pray for him. Weeks of earnest prayer that he should get well seemed already to have failed. I couldn't even think how to quote scripture to him without the words seeming false or empty.

But after Ken's death I learned that the hospice staff had controlled Ken's pain and sickness, and I realised that God had heard my prayers all along. My friend had died in peace.

God is reliable; his word is truth. I just needed to learn to trust him.

Prayer: *Dear Lord, help us always to listen to your leading and to trust you when we feel unsure of ourselves. Amen*

Thought for the day: Today I will listen for God's voice.

M.S. Foster (Cheshire, England)

Calm amid Chaos

Read Luke 21:25–28

'When these things begin to take place, stand up and raise your heads, because your redemption is drawing near.'
Luke 21:28 (NRSV)

News of chaos in communities around the world tempts me to live in fear. Threats of violent attacks, natural disasters, war, disease, famine and financial crises alarm me. When I have faced one fear another takes its place. I wonder, how can I protect myself? How can I overcome my fears?

When these concerns start to overwhelm me, I think of Jesus' words in today's quoted scripture verse. I am comforted as I turn from the chaos and look to Jesus—my redemption—who calms my fears.

We may struggle with concerns about our family, health or finances. We may live in an area with daily violence due to war or crime. Disease and natural disasters pose a constant threat. When we experience any of these things we can remember the promise of redemption. We can look first to Jesus as a source of comfort, hope and joy in the midst of chaos.

Prayer: *Dear Lord Jesus, thank you for your constant presence. Give us the strength to look to you first when we experience threats to our well-being. Amen*

Thought for the day: I will remember to keep Jesus first at all times.

Gerald Bauer (Ohio, US)

Fourth Sunday of Advent

Read Hebrews 2:10–18

Behold, a virgin shall be with child, and shall bring forth a son, and they shall call his name Emmanuel, which being interpreted is, God with us.
Matthew 1:23 (KJV)

Although Christmas is a time of joy for many, it can also be a time of sorrow. Some people experience isolation and loneliness in the face of broken relationships or the painful absence of loved ones who have passed away. Others struggle with the financial demands they feel in this season.

Still, we find great joy at Christmastime when we consider its true meaning, 'God with us'. Throughout the Bible, God demonstrates love for all people. Jesus Christ's birth, life and death show humanity the true nature and depth of God's love. He showed profound love by sending Jesus to be 'God with us'. He understands our hopes, joys, fears, pains and struggles because he was born among us. While particular circumstances may seem cause for despair, Christmas reminds us that God loves us and is with us.

Prayer: *Holy and Incarnate One, thank you for living among us. Remind us that you understand all that we will ever experience. Amen*

Thought for the day: Christ understands all that I experience.

Jonathan Emerson-Pierce (Ontario, Canada)

The Perfect Parent

Read Deuteronomy 32:7–11

[The Lord said] 'I carried you on eagles' wings and brought you to myself.'
Exodus 19:4 (NIV)

When I was pregnant with my first child, someone told me that becoming a parent for the first time would deepen my understanding of God's love for me. They were right. I've always carefully watched over my son like a mother hen, nurturing him and keeping him safe because I love him dearly: from the first day when I held my baby carefully, supporting his head, to the first time I held his hand as he came down the slide, to the first time I told him to jump to me in the water where I waited to catch him.

Deuteronomy describes God 'Like an eagle protecting its nest, hovering over its young' (32:11, CEB). From this, I learn that the good qualities of my parenting—my unconditional love, my protective instincts, my desire to make sacrifices for my children's sake—are God-given gifts.

God's love is deeper, stronger and more perfect than a human parent's love could ever be. As God's beloved children, we can lean into that love and receive help to be the people he calls us to be.

Prayer: *Gracious God, thank you for your deep and unconditional love. Help us to love others the way you love us. In Jesus' name we pray. Amen*

Thought for the day: God is our perfect parent who shows us how to love.

Jayna Richardson (Arkansas, US)

The Aroma of Christ

Read 2 Corinthians 2:14–16

Thanks be to God, who in Christ always leads us in triumphal procession, and through us spreads in every place the fragrance that comes from knowing him.
2 Corinthians 2:14 (NRSV)

As I was working in my garden one day, I noticed one winter rose starting to bloom. Since I knew that the cold would kill it anyway, I clipped it off and brought it indoors. Over the next few days, the rose unfolded and its beautiful scent filled our living room.

The flower's aroma took me back to childhood visits to Grandma's house in Northern California. Her home was filled with the scent of roses. I remembered Grandpa snoozing in his armchair and their feisty little Yorkshire terrier running around the house. Among all these memories the aroma of roses was the strongest.

We've been created to spread the fragrance of the knowledge of God in every place (2 Corinthians 2:14). We spread the fragrance that comes from knowing Christ when we imitate his example of love and sacrificial service (Ephesians 5:1–2). As the scent of a rose conjures a pleasant memory, our lives of service are meant to remind people of God's love and care for them. What could be more pleasing to our Creator?

Prayer: *Dear Lord, help us to be joyful imitators of Jesus Christ. May our lives give off the fragrance of Christ to those who may need a reminder of how much you care for them. Amen*

Thought for the day: What am I doing to remind others of God's love?

Timothy Austin (Turkey)

Living in Harmony

Read John 13:33–35

'I give you a new commandment, that you love one another. Just as I have loved you, you also should love one another.'
John 13:34 (NRSV)

My daughter and granddaughter met a woman named Sophia who needed somewhere to live that was nearer to her place of employment. After discussing cost and responsibilities, they reached an agreement for Sophia to live with them.

Sophia is an Orthodox Jew, while our daughter and granddaughter are Christians. Yet a trusting and loving friendship has come from sharing their religious faiths and backgrounds. Certain areas of the kitchen have been set apart for Sophia to prepare and store her kosher food. As they celebrate their religious holidays, they share knowledge of these holidays with one another. This has led to many good conversations and deeper understanding.

My daughter and granddaughter have had an opportunity to enjoy a rewarding friendship by following Jesus' example and his command for us to love our neighbours as ourselves (see Matthew 22:39). By sharing and respecting others' beliefs, we can build relationships filled with harmony, love and trust.

Prayer: *Dear God of all, help us to understand and show love to everyone so that we may share your peace with those around us. Amen*

Thought for the day: With God's help, I can live in unity and peace with others.

Shirley Cottle (North Carolina, US)

A Time for Everything

Read Ecclesiastes 3:1–8

There is a time for everything, and a season for every activity under the heavens… a time to weep and a time to laugh, a time to mourn and a time to dance.

Ecclesiastes 3:1, 4 (NIV)

When my nephew called to tell me that my 27-year-old niece had died suddenly, my whole body began to shake. She had been like a daughter to me. During the agonising days after her death, I wondered if I would ever smile again. I wanted to be transported many years down the road where I hoped the pain might be less. My heart was broken and I was not sure it could ever be repaired.

Today's reading from Ecclesiastes reminds us that some seasons of our lives bring sorrow, but some bring joy. Sometimes, when we are in the midst of heartbreak, we feel that our lives will be filled with unrelenting pain. We find it hard to imagine a less painful time in the future. We feel trapped in sorrow with no hope.

I have found that although I still carry sadness about my niece's death, I am now able to smile again and enjoy those blessings that God has so graciously given to me. God's word gives us hope for another season after sorrow, a season of joy and celebration— reminding us that he will walk with us in both seasons and bring healing to go forward. We will not always stay in that season of grief; we will be able to rejoice again.

Prayer: *Dear God, thank you that even in seasons of deepest sorrow you are nearby and your love will see us through. Give us hope for the future, so that we may persevere. Amen*

Thought for the day: Because God is with me, even in grief I can have hope (see 1 Thessalonians 4:13).

Lin Daniels (Massachusetts, US)

God Hears Our Prayers

Read Romans 8:18–27

The Spirit helps us in our weakness. We do not know what we ought to pray for, but the Spirit himself intercedes for us through wordless groans.
Romans 8:26 (NIV)

Our Bible study leader makes a list of our prayer requests so that we can pray for one another's specific needs. I recently asked the group to pray for God's help for me to become a friend to my ex-husband. Then I began to worry that I was praying for the wrong thing and that I had encouraged several other people to pray amiss as well.

Troubled about this situation, I took my fears to God. The words from Romans 8:26 came to mind and reassured me that I can trust him to sort out my prayers. God continues to bring about changes in our relationship. I pray for his will to be done and for my heart to be willing to follow where he leads me.

When I don't know what to pray for, I can trust that the Holy Spirit will intercede.

Prayer: *Thank you, God, for hearing our prayers always, even when we struggle to pray. Thank you for Jesus Christ, in whose name we pray: 'Our Father which art in heaven, Hallowed be thy name. Thy kingdom come. Thy will be done, as in heaven, so in earth. Give us day by day our daily bread. And forgive us our sins; for we also forgive every one that is indebted to us. And lead us not into temptation; but deliver us from evil.'* Amen*

Thought for the day: God hears us even when we do not know what to pray for.

Connie L. Miller (Indiana, US)

* Luke 11:2–4 (KJV)

Christmas Eve

Read Matthew 10:1–8

Create in me a clean heart, O God, and put a new and right spirit within me.
Psalm 51:10 (NRSV)

I conducted the Christmas morning service at a country church in New South Wales. Following the service I shook hands with people at the door. A neatly dressed young man with long blond hair greeted me by calling me 'Mr Mac'. I did not recognise him and he said, 'Have you forgotten me? I was the worst kid in your scripture class at school.' I remembered and then called him by name. We talked for a while, and he told me that he was grateful for my putting up with him. He had made a decision to follow Christ and had become secretary of the student Christian movement at his university.

I congratulated him on his decision and wished him well in his future studies and as a Christian. I learned a valuable lesson that day: we may never know what awaits those who hear God's word. When we share the messages of the Bible, we can rely on God to use our constant proclamation of faith to do the converting and the calling.

Prayer: *God of compassion, help us to see the potential you see in others and to be an example for those around us. Amen*

Thought for the day: Today I will thank someone who has shaped my faith.

Jim MacLean (Queensland, Australia)

Christmas Day

Read Luke 2:8–16

[Jesus said] 'Where two or three are gathered in my name, I'm there with them.'
Matthew 18:20 (CEB)

As Americans living in Bangladesh, my husband and I longed to be with other Christians for the Christmas celebration. Since we were too far away to travel home, we chose to visit London. On a sunny but crisp Christmas morning, we arrived at the site of our church denomination in London, only a short distance from Westminster Abbey.

The 100-year-old church had soaring ceilings, beautiful windows and creaky wooden floors. The congregation was not large, but the minister who conducted the service was so cordial and enthusiastic that we were humbled and grateful to be there. It had been so long since we had been in a place of Christian worship. As we sang carols and listened to the Christmas story, tears filled our eyes.

We still longed for our families, but we could feel the presence of God there in that London congregation—looking after two homesick souls, so far away from all that was familiar. Afterwards, as we walked through St James's Park, we were so moved that we could not speak. Even though we were in London and longing to be in the United States, our thoughts were in Bethlehem. My husband and I realised that it didn't matter where we were located when we prayed. We were still in God's care.

Prayer: *Dear Lord, bless those who show the Christmas spirit to the homesick and befriend the needy. Help us to reflect your love to all. Amen*

Thought for the day: Wherever we are, we can celebrate the presence of God and the gift of Jesus Christ.

Joanne Emmons (Oklahoma, US)

A Firm Foundation

Read 1 Corinthians 3:1–13

Each one should build with care.
1 Corinthians 3:10 (NIV)

It was Christmas. Everyone had unwrapped their gifts and discarded wrapping paper covered the floor. My son examined a little wooden truck filled with different-sized bricks. He began to build, but the tower of bricks soon fell over. Being a young child, he didn't realise that because his blocks were not built in the right order, his tower would not stand.

Whatever is built needs balance and a firm foundation, and building up a church as the body of Christ is no exception. Our basic priorities are to help people to lay the foundations of their faith in Jesus as Lord, and to provide guidance for the future. We all have a part to play, using whatever gifts we have to encourage and serve people (see 1 Corinthians 12:4–7).

'Each one should build with care,' said Paul. Whether it is building a church or building our Christian faith, with Jesus as our cornerstone our priorities are in the right place.

Prayer: *Lord, we ask for your guidance in building up our church. Amen*

Thought for the day: Today I will play my part in encouraging and serving.

Pauline Pullan (Yorkshire, England)

Seek and Call

Read Psalm 139:1–18

[The Lord says] 'When you search for me, you will find me; if you seek me with all your heart."
Jeremiah 29:13 (NRSV)

I remember a time when I was seeking the Lord for guidance regarding a job opportunity. Every aspect of the position seemed right except for one: my wife and I would have to move to Southeast Asia, away from our family, friends, church and country. I prayed, fasted, studied the Bible and sought advice from trusted friends. For months I diligently sought the Lord's direction. I truly wanted to know God's will, but in the course of my seeking I also found myself asking, 'Do I truly want to know God?'

I realised that God wants to be sought not only for answers but for a deeper relationship. For me, this type of seeking extends beyond my normal daily prayers. It requires an immersion in God's word at a level that allows inspiration to overwhelm me with truth and awe.

God is always present. Even so, scripture still encourages us to seek him. Reading Psalm 139 and Isaiah 55 can help us to ponder the majesty, glory and goodness of God and to realise that he who formed us is great and always present. Such meditation and reflection can help us to go beyond seeking answers to our questions or solutions to our problems to find a true relationship with him.

Prayer: *Dear God, help us to seek you with our whole heart so that we may honour you all of our days. Amen*

Thought for the day: Today I will seek a deeper relationship with God.

Gary A. Miller (California, US)

The Bruised Reed

Read Isaiah 42:1–9

A bruised reed he will not break, and a smouldering wick he will not snuff out. In faithfulness he will bring forth justice.
Isaiah 42:3 (NIV)

Early civilisations developed methods to transform reeds into paper and papyrus, and also to weave them into baskets, mats and rope. Reeds were functional and beautiful. In contrast, a bruised reed was not beautiful and appeared to be useless.

Similarly, a bruise on our skin is a visible sign of injury. We can see the bruise, but the damage is deeper. I am bruised because I bear the mark of sexual abuse. The words from Isaiah quoted above brought me peace and understanding; Jesus is a gentle and compassionate Saviour. Just as God's servant noticed the one bruised reed among the millions that flanked the Nile River, Jesus noticed me and recognised that I was fragile.

Jesus understands loneliness and physical pain. He has felt the sting of injustice. With empathy and understanding, Jesus bends down to us and tends the bruised reed. He will not snuff out our faith even when it flickers. He promises also that, in time, he will faithfully bring forth justice. Because of Jesus, we may be bruised, but we are not broken.

Prayer: *Dear Jesus, thank you for understanding our pain and for healing and transforming us. Amen*

Thought for the day: Jesus is the suffering servant who has experienced our pain.

Jennifer Dudding (New South Wales, Australia)

The Best Dwelling Place

Read John 14:1–7

In my Father's house are many mansions: if it were not so, I would have told you. I go to prepare a place for you.
John 14:2 (KJV)

I have lived in many different places since my parents, my brothers and I left Latvia to escape Communism. On our journey to freedom, we lived for a short time in Poland and Germany. Later we were fortunate enough to emigrate to the United States.

All I can remember from my home in Latvia is the grand piano in the large living room where my aunt filled the space with music. One day when I searched online for the address of my childhood home, I discovered that the house was for sale. I was able to view the many furnished rooms with their hardwood floors.

As I thought about the possibility of once again living in my childhood home, I remembered the verse quoted above. Then I realised that this was not a realistic dream, and I began to turn my focus away from where I might live on earth to where I will live when I die. God has taken care of me here on earth, and I know that whatever happens to me, he watches over me. The place Jesus Christ has prepared for me is even better than my beloved home here or in Latvia. Every day, I can thank the Lord for this promise.

Prayer: *God of salvation, thank you for caring for us and for offering us the gift of eternal life with you. Amen*

Thought for the day: Our heavenly home is better than any earthly home.

Christa Eckert Blum (Ohio, US)

As a Little Child

Read Luke 18:15–17
In Christ Jesus you are all children of God through faith.
Galatians 3:26 (NRSV)

The family table was set, and we were all excited about beginning the meal. Instead of blessing the food with our usual prayer, we decided to share something for which we were thankful. Some people said friends; some said the food; others said family, home or community. When it was five-year-old Lila's turn she said, 'I am thankful for God and Jesus.' After she had spoken we all realised that she had reminded us of our greatest blessing.

There was nothing more for us to say but 'Amen'.

The Bible encourages us to become like children because this is the best way to receive God's promises. Children are often eager to learn from adults, but we adults can all learn from children how to accept things through faith—for as today's scripture verse states, 'In Christ Jesus you are all children of God through faith.'

Prayer: *Dear Lord, thank you for children who show us our greatest blessings and show us how to love you better. Amen*

Thought for the day: How can I receive the kingdom of God like a child?

James R. Hayes (Tennessee, US)

These Are the Days!

Read Philippians 3:12–14

*'Look, I have set before you an open door, which no one is able to shut.
I know that you have but little power, and yet you have kept my word
and have not denied my name.'*
Revelation 3:8 (NRSV)

One of my favourite television shows from the 1970s always opened
with the two main characters sitting at a piano singing, 'Those Were
the Days'. As I think about this song, I realise that it is easy for us to
look back and idolise the 'good old days'. But scripture challenges
us to sing, 'These are the days!'

To the church in Philadelphia, John was instructed to write,
'Look, I have set before you an open door, which no one is able to
shut. I know that you have but little power, and yet you have kept
my word and have not denied my name' (Revelation 3:8). Here and
now we are called to celebrate God's presence. Here and now we
are called to embrace what God is doing in our lives. He has placed
before us open doors of opportunity. We don't want to miss them
by looking back or because we are afraid of what lies on the other
side of the threshold. Instead, we can follow the apostle Paul's
example: 'I do this one thing: I forget about the things behind me
and reach out for the things ahead of me' (Philippians 3:13, CEB).
Like Paul, we can celebrate and embrace what God is doing and is
going to do in our lives.

Prayer: *Loving God, strengthen us to press forward in faith, knowing
that you are showing us open doors of opportunity. Lead, guide and
direct us by your Spirit. Amen*

Thought for the day: Today I will celebrate and embrace what God
is doing in my life.

Christopher Yopp (Virginia, US)

Small Group Questions

Wednesday 7 September

1. The writer of the meditation mentions Romans 7:15: 'I do not understand what I do. For what I want to do I do not do, but what I hate I do' (NIV). What does this verse mean to you?

2. Do you have any symbols that you use to let others know you are a Christian? If so, what are they? What is it that you want people to know when they see these symbols?

3. The writer says, 'I am reminded that while I am less than the shining example I strive to be, I will continue to strive. That is the Christian's walk.' In what ways do you relate to this statement?

4. What do others see when they look at you? Is this what you want them to see?

5. In what ways could you be a more Christlike example to others today?

Wednesday 14 September

1. Are there any scripture passages that you have memorised? If so, what are they? When did you memorise them, and what was the process like for you?

2. How does your church encourage you and others to engage with scripture? How do others in your community set an example of connection to scripture? Describe someone whose study of scripture you admire or would like to emulate.

3. Do you have other practices aside from memorisation that help keep you connected to scripture? If so, what are they?

4. The writer of this meditation says, 'God's word is something I'll never give up. Who knows when I might be called upon to perform an impromptu concert?' What does she mean by this? When have you called upon scripture in an unexpected moment?

5. Which word or phrase from today's Bible reading caught your attention? Why this particular word or phrase? What is this scripture passage saying to you today?

Wednesday 21 September

1. What prevents you from finding time to spend with God in prayer or some other spiritual practice? What would it look like for you to make time for God with the regularity of the exchange student in this meditation?

2. Where and at what times during the day do you pray? Why do you pray at these particular times and places and not others?

3. The writer of the meditation describes prayer as a 'tremendous privilege'. In what ways do you experience prayer as a 'tremendous privilege'? How else might you describe your experience of prayer?

4. Have you ever asked God for something in prayer and received an answer immediately or shortly thereafter? What did you pray for and what was God's answer? What was the experience like for you? If you have not had such an experience, how do stories like today's meditation make you feel?

5. Where or from whom have you learned the most about how to pray and what to pray for? Are there specific books, other resources or teachers that influenced you and encouraged you in your prayer life? If so, what are they? How did they change the way you pray?

Wednesday 28 September

1. Have you ever had an experience when someone treated you generously even though you probably didn't deserve it? What was the experience like for you? What did it teach you about fairness?

2. Have you ever had an experience similar to that in the parable, where you were the twelve-hour worker but were rewarded the same as the one-hour worker? How did this make you feel? What did you take away from this experience?

3. What do you think about the writer's last statement, 'That's not fair; that's grace'? Can grace ever be fair? Why or why not?

4. When thinking about grace, are there other parables that come to mind? If so, which ones? What do these parables say about grace?

5. Is there anyone in your personal life or community to whom you need to extend grace? In what ways, big or small, can you show grace to this person today?

Wednesday 5 October

1. Has there ever been a time in your life of faith when you have pretended to follow Jesus or 'gone through the motions'? What circumstances surrounded this period in your life, and what was the experience like for you? Looking back, what did you learn?

2. What does it mean to you when Jesus says we are to follow him and fish for people? What does this look like in your daily life, activities and relationships? Is this a challenging or an empowering invitation for you?

3. To what can you give your whole heart today? A community project? A small-group Bible study? Something else?

4. What does ministry look like to you? Is there more to ministry than being a preacher at a church? If so, what is it? In what ways can you minister to others without being a preacher?

5. Think of someone from your life whose strong faith and Christ-like actions inspire and encourage you. What can you draw from this person's example that might help you when tempted to go through the motions? How would you encourage others who feel they are going through the motions of faith?

Wednesday 12 October

1. In what ways do you identify with the Israelites? How would you have reacted if God promised you something but it didn't come immediately?

2. Recall a time in your life when things got worse before they got better. What was going on in your life at the time? Having had this experience, will you approach your next obstacle differently?

3. Do you think that encountering obstacles may be part of God's plan for us? Why or why not?

4. What obstacles are you faced with today? What challenges do these obstacles present? What opportunities? Where do you sense God's presence in these circumstances?

5. The writer mentions four biblical characters whose struggles got worse before they got better—Moses, Joseph, Abraham and Paul. Can you think of other figures in the Bible who endured significant challenges but who went on to do great things for God? Who are they? What in their stories do you connect with? What do you learn from them?

Wednesday 19 October

1. Do you have any specific practices you observe before reading scripture? What are they? How do these practices prepare you for reading scripture and what benefit are they to you as you approach God through the Bible?

2. What distractions of daily life do you find yourself dealing with most often when trying to turn your attention to God? Why do you think these distractions—often nothing more than minor annoyances—are so powerful?

3. Do you find meditation or quiet prayer easy or difficult? Are there certain places or environments where it is easier for you to meditate or pray than others? Describe them.

4. How often would you say you are able to focus your attention entirely on reading scripture? Why is it important to read God's word with our full attention?

5. In what ways is reading scripture on one's own different from reading scripture as part of a small group or faith community? Are there advantages and disadvantages in each? If so, what are they?

Wednesday 26 October

1. Do you think it irritates God when we ask for the same thing over and over again? Why or why not? Do you think God cares about how we pray or how often we pray? If so, in what ways does he care?

2. What characters in the Bible can you think of who pestered God? What do their stories teach us about our prayers and our relationship to him?

3. Think of a time in your life when you asked God several times for something and expected that he would give it to you. How did he answer this prayer? Did you get what you had been asking for?

4. Why do you think it is that sometimes God answers our prayers immediately and in a way we recognise, and at other times does not? Have you ever asked God for something and he said no? How did this make you feel and what did you learn from the experience? Did it change the way you pray? If so, how?

5. What does God want from us regarding prayer? Do you believe that there are certain ways we must pray in order for God to hear our prayers? Do you think he ever ignores our prayers?

Wednesday 2 November

1. Reflect on a time when you were uncertain where God was leading you. What was occurring in your life at the time? What was that experience like for you? How did this experience affect your faith? How did you seek God's guidance during this time?

2. Do you think detours or sidetracks in our lives sometimes can have a larger meaning? Why or why not? What scripture passages help you to answer this question?

3. The writer of today's meditation mentions Moses leading the Israelites to the promised land. What other characters in the Bible can you think of who experienced long and difficult journeys not knowing exactly where God was leading them? Which of these people do you most identify with and why?

4. If you were to describe your life journey using only one word, what would it be and why?

5. Where do you think God is leading you today? How will you continue to discern God's call? What will be your next steps to following God's leading?

Wednesday 9 November

1. What have you learned about God that you didn't expect to learn? How and when did you learn this? How can you help others to learn this about God?

2. Describe your relationship with God. How has your relationship with him changed over time? How do you hope your relationship with him will change in the coming year? What will you do to work toward change?

3. In today's meditation, John writes, 'God wants to be part of my life at all times.' Do you feel this is true for you? How do you know? How do you strive to make God part of your life each day?

4. How does your church or faith community talk about prayer? Is prayer something everyone does or only certain people? Is prayer something reserved for 'emergencies' or a way to connect with God and build faith at any time?

5. How can you make prayer a part of your daily life? What prayer ministries, groups or practices might you explore to deepen your prayer life?

Wednesday 16 November

1. Why do you think Job's friends questioned God in the midst of Job's difficult circumstances? Have you ever questioned God when a family member or friend was going through hard times?

2. Who do you identify with most in Job's story, Job or his friends? Why?

3. Has there ever been a time when you said the 'wrong' thing to a person experiencing grief? What helped you to recognise your mistake? How did you learn from this experience?

4. Has someone said the 'wrong' thing to you in a moment of grief? What did they say? What could they have said that would have been more helpful?

5. Do you see any value in sitting silently with a person who is enduring a difficult time? If so, what is it? What do you find challenging or rewarding about doing this?

Wednesday 23 November

1. What is your pattern for spending time with God? What practices, readings and times of day seem to work best for you? What have you tried that has not worked for you?

2. Do you feel that you spend as much time with God as you should? If not, what keeps you from spending more time with him?

3. The writer of the meditation says, 'I want to come hungry and thirsty to the feast of love God continually spreads for all.' In what ways do you identify with this statement?

4. What scripture passages can you think of that speak to the importance of spending time with God?

5. What role does discipline play in your spiritual life? What would it look like for you to be more disciplined in your spiritual life?

Wednesday 30 November

1. How did you react to or identify with today's meditation? Describe any similar experience you have had. What was most powerful about this story?

2. Recall a time when a person or group prayed for you. If you knew about the prayers at the time, what effect did knowing others were praying for you have on you?

3. Has there ever been a time when you have prayed continuously for something but your prayer has gone unanswered? What helps you persevere in prayer even when your prayers go unanswered?

4. Today's Thought for the day says, 'The prayers of others are gifts from God.' What does this statement mean to you? How have you experienced this?

5. Who in your congregation or community needs your prayers today? How will you let them know you are praying for them?

Wednesday 7 December

1. When was the last time you witnessed a Christian action that had a lasting impact on you? What was it? Why did it make such an impression on you? What has this experience inspired you to do?

2. When have you given freely to another person? What does scripture say about giving freely of ourselves? What verses come to mind?

3. The writer says the teenagers' actions helped her see more clearly 'the power of Christ's love to transform each of us'. What helps you see more clearly the transformative love of Christ?

4. Recall an act of kindness shown to you for which you were very grateful. What was it, and what was the experience like for you? How have you tried to show kindness to others in light of this experience?

5. Think of individuals within your congregation or community who are in need. Name some specific acts of kindness that you can show them today.

Wednesday 14 December

1. What passages in the Bible do you struggle with most? What passages would you omit and why? Why do you think these passages were included? Why is it important to wrestle with these difficult passages?

2. Describe a moment or experience that changed your feelings about Christmas. What emotions and memories shape your experience of this season now?

3. Michael writes that this passage reminds him that God brings hope to seemingly hopeless situations. What other passages in the Bible help you to remember the hope God offers?

4. Name some of the hopeless places in the world today. Take a moment to pray for these people and situations.

5. How does your church acknowledge the mixed emotions of the Christmas season? Name some ways you might support those who are grieving, hurting or lonely this season.

Wednesday 21 December

1. Recall a time when you lived with or shared a house with someone who was not a family member. What was the best thing about this situation? What did you learn about yourself or others from this experience?

2. What is your experience of people of different faiths? Have you had the opportunity to befriend someone of another faith? What was challenging or surprising about that friendship?

3. Where and how do you learn about other religious traditions or other Christian denominations? How does learning about another person's faith help to strengthen your own?

4. What other faith traditions are present in your city or community? How does your church or faith group interact with other faith communities? How might you encourage conversation between these groups?

5. Shirley lifts up the example in today's meditation as a way of 'following Jesus' example and his command for us to love our neighbours as ourselves'. Name some other ways you can love your neighbours in the coming weeks.

Wednesday 28 December

1. Reeds from the Nile were useful for making paper even when they were broken. Suggest objects that might be reused beyond their original design. In what ways can you use the broken pieces in your life to create something new and useful?

2. Recall a time when you were bruised or injured. What was the cause of your injury? How did this injury affect your life in the short term and in the long term?

3. How does your faith inform the way you deal with hardship, grief or injury? What spiritual practices, people or Bible verses give you comfort when you are suffering?

4. How does your church or community care for those who have been injured or abused? Name some specific people or ministries that care for those who are suffering. How can you help others to find comfort or healing?

5. Does it help you to know that Jesus has experienced suffering? If so, how? If not, why not?

Share it with a friend!

We recently conducted a survey to see what our readers think of *The Upper Room* and why they read it. It was encouraging to hear of the positive impact *The Upper Room* is having on your lives. Often it started because someone recommended, shared or gave a gift of *The Upper Room* to you.

Would you considering sharing a copy with a friend or family member?

Here are some ways you could share your experience of BRF's Bible reading notes:

- **Recommend:** We'd like to encourage you to talk about *The Upper Room* and the readings that have particularly spoken to you. Maybe someone will consider picking up a copy, so that it can have a positive effect on their life too.

- **Give it:** It's really easy to set up a gift subscription for any of BRF's Bible reading notes. To find out more, just go to our web page (**www.biblereadingnotes.org.uk/subscriptions**) or speak to our Customer Services team on +44 (0)1865 319700.

- **Start a group:** If you order five or more copies of our Bible reading notes, you can set up a group subscription and save money, as you pay no postage and packaging charges.

- **Donate a copy:** When you've finished with your copy, give it to your local church or to someone who can make use of it.

Journal page

Journal page

Journal page

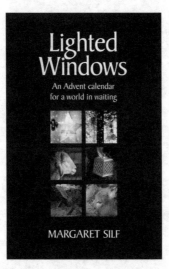

The birth of a baby invariably stirs deep wells of hope in the human heart. Perhaps in this generation, things will get better. Perhaps this child will make a difference. As we approach the Christmas season we prepare to celebrate the coming to earth of someone who really does make a difference. At this season the 'windows' of our human experience can change from rows of faceless panes, perhaps grimy with dirt, into lighted windows that open up new possibilities and coax us into a place where rejoicing might be possible.

Lighted Windows
An Advent calendar for a world in waiting
Margaret Silf
978 0 85746 432 3 £7.99
brf.org.uk

In a series of pithy, poignant and profound readings, this book explores the intersection of faith and life. Spotting parables in the everyday, it equips readers to explore whether they might be bumping into God without realising it. Heartening and often humorous, it applies biblical truth in a way that both fascinates and liberates.

Could This Be God?
Bumping into God in the everyday
Brian Harris
978 0 85746 500 9 £8.99
brf.org.uk

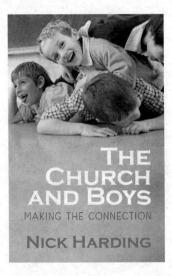

Why are boys so under-represented in churches? Why do churches find it so difficult to cater for boys? What would help boys in church to grow into mature men of faith? This uniquely inspiring book by Nick Harding spells out the problem and encourages churches to see it in missional terms. The book includes resources, suggestions and ideas to help boys connect better with the church, with the Bible and with the Christian faith.

The Church and Boys
Making the connection
Nick Harding
978 0 85746 509 2 £9.99
brf.org.uk

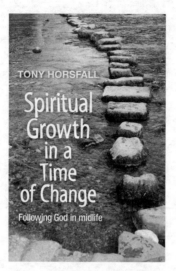

Midlife—our 40s and 50s—can be some of the most important years of our lives in spiritual terms. They are also times of change, which can include turbulent emotional transitions as we encounter a range of challenging personal issues. Tony Horsfall not only addresses a number of such issues—from facing up to the past to renegotiating relationships—but explores how to navigate a spiritual journey through these years, leading to deeper faith and a closer walk with God.

Spiritual Growth in a Time of Change
Following God in midlife
Tony Horsfall
978 0 85746 435 4 £7.99
brf.org.uk

How to encourage Bible reading in your church

BRF has been helping individuals connect with the Bible for over 90 years. We want to support churches as they seek to encourage church members into regular Bible reading.

Order a Bible reading resources pack
This pack is designed to give your church the tools to publicise our Bible reading notes. It includes:

- Sample Bible reading notes for your congregation to try.
- Publicity resources, including a poster.
- A church magazine feature about Bible reading notes.

The pack is free, but we welcome a £5 donation to cover the cost of postage. If you require a pack to be sent outside the UK or require a specific number of sample Bible reading notes, please contact us for postage costs. More information about what the current pack contains is available on our website.

How to order and find out more
- Visit **biblereadingnotes.org.uk/for-churches**
- Telephone BRF on +44 (0)1865 319700 between 9.15 am and 5.30 pm.
- Write to us at BRF, 15 The Chambers, Vineyard, Abingdon OX14 3FE.

Keep informed about our latest initiatives
We are continuing to develop resources to help churches encourage people into regular Bible reading, wherever they are on their journey. Join our email list at **www.biblereadingnotes.org.uk/helpingchurches** to stay informed about the latest initiatives that your church could benefit from.

Introduce a friend to our notes
We can send information about our notes and current prices for you to pass on. Please contact us.

Subscriptions

The Upper Room is published in January, May and September.

Individual subscriptions

The subscription rate for orders for 4 or fewer copies includes postage and packing:

The Upper Room annual individual subscription   £16.20

Group subscriptions

Orders for 5 copies or more, sent to ONE address, are post free:
The Upper Room annual group subscription   £13.05

Please do not send payment with order for a group subscription. We will send an invoice with your first order.

Please note that the annual billing period for group subscriptions runs from 1 May to 30 April.

Copies of the notes may also be obtained from Christian bookshops.

Single copies of *The Upper Room* cost £4.35.

Prices valid until 30 April 2017.

Giant print version

The Upper Room is available in giant print for the visually impaired, from:

Torch Trust for the Blind
Torch House
Torch Way
Northampton Road
Market Harborough
LE16 9HL

Tel: +44 (0)1858 438260
torchtrust.org

THE UPPER ROOM: INDIVIDUAL/GIFT SUBSCRIPTION FORM

**All our Bible reading notes can be ordered online by visiting
biblereadingnotes.org.uk/subscriptions**

☐ I would like to take out a subscription myself (complete your name and address details once)
☐ I would like to give a gift subscription (please provide both names and addresses)

Title .... First name/initials .... Surname ....
Address ....
.... Postcode ....
Telephone .... Email ....
Gift subscription name ....
Gift subscription address ....
.... Postcode ....

Gift message (20 words max. or include your own gift card):

....
....

Please send **The Upper Room** beginning with the January 2017 / May 2017 / September 2017
issue (delete as appropriate):

Annual individual subscription ☐ £16.20   Total enclosed £ ....

Please keep me informed about BRF's books and resources ☐ by email ☐ by post
Please keep me informed about the wider work of BRF ☐ by email ☐ by post

Method of payment

☐ Cheque (made payable to BRF) ☐ MasterCard / Visa

Card no. ☐☐☐☐ ☐☐☐☐ ☐☐☐☐ ☐☐☐☐

Valid from ☐☐/☐☐   Expires ☐☐/☐☐

Security code* ☐☐☐   *Last 3 digits on the reverse of the card
ESSENTIAL IN ORDER TO PROCESS THE PAYMENT

Please return to:
BRF, 15 The Chambers, Vineyard, Abingdon OX14 3FE | enquiries@brf.org.uk
To read our terms and find out about cancelling your order, please visit brfonline.org.uk/terms

The Bible Reading Fellowship is a Registered Charity (233280)

UR0316

THE UPPER ROOM: GROUP SUBSCRIPTION FORM

> **All our Bible reading notes can be ordered online by visiting biblereadingnotes.org.uk/subscriptions**

☐ Please send me .... copies of *The Upper Room* January 2017 / May 2017 / September 2017 issue (delete as appropriate)

Title .... First name/initials .... Surname ....

Address ....

.... Postcode ....

Telephone .... Email ....

Please do not send payment with this order. We will send an invoice with your first order.

Christian bookshops: All good Christian bookshops stock BRF publications. For your nearest stockist, please contact BRF.

Telephone: The BRF office is open between 9.15 and 17.30. To place your order, telephone +44 (0)1865 319700.

Online: brf.org.uk

☐ Please send me a Bible reading resources pack to encourage Bible reading in my church

 Please return to:
BRF, 15 The Chambers, Vineyard, Abingdon OX14 3FE | enquiries@brf.org.uk
To read our terms and find out about cancelling your order, please visit **brfonline.org.uk/terms**

The Bible Reading Fellowship is a Registered Charity (233280)

To order

Online: **brfonline.org.uk**
Tel.: +44 (0)1865 319700
Mon–Fri 9.15–17.30

Delivery times within the UK are normally
15 working days. Prices are correct at the time of
going to press but may change without prior notice.

Title	Price	Qty	Total
Lighted Windows	7.99		
Could This Be God?	8.99		
The Church and Boys	9.99		
Spiritual Growth in a Time of Change	7.99		

POSTAGE AND PACKING CHARGES			
Order value	UK	Europe	Rest of world
Under £7.00	£1.25	£3.00	£5.50
£7.00–£29.99	£2.25	£5.50	£10.00
£30.00 and over	FREE	Prices on request	

Total value of books	
Postage and packing	
Donation	
Total for this order	

**Please complete
in BLOCK CAPITALS**

Title .... First name/initials .... Surname...

Address...

.... Postcode ....

Acc. No. .... Telephone ....

Email...

Please keep me informed about BRF's books and resources ❏ by email ❏ by post
Please keep me informed about the wider work of BRF ❏ by email ❏ by post

Method of payment

❏ Cheque (made payable to BRF) ❏ MasterCard / Visa

Card no. ☐☐☐☐ ☐☐☐☐ ☐☐☐☐ ☐☐☐☐

Valid from ☐M☐M ☐Y☐Y Expires ☐M☐M ☐Y☐Y Security code* ☐☐☐

*Last 3 digits on the reverse of the card

Signature* .... Date .... /............ /............
*ESSENTIAL IN ORDER TO PROCESS YOUR ORDER

The Bible Reading Fellowship Gift Aid Declaration

giftaid it

Please return to: BRF, 15 The Chambers, Vineyard, Abingdon OX14 3FE | enquiries@brf.org.uk
To read our terms and find out about cancelling your order, please visit **brfonline.org.uk/terms** **UR0316**